GROUND ZERO
DISCLOSURE: UFOS

By Clyde Lewis

GROUND ZERO DISCLOSURE: UFOS

Published by

PARANOIA Publishing
http://www.paranoiamagazine.com

The views expressed in this book are those of the author and do not necessarily represent the views of the Anomalies Network LLC, PARANOIA Publishing or its affiliates.

SIGHTING : THE CAUSE FUZZY LOGIC, ALIEN GRAVES, AND CHINESE LANTERNS

Two objects caught on video darting in front of a giant Arizona sandstorm have created a new keen interest in UFO's on the Internet. I watched the footage after a long hot day at the zoo and I admit I was spooked by what looked like to saucer like craft moving out of the huge cloud of dust. They looked very much like the classic UFOs seen in other footage.

The unidentified flying objects were seen in the giant storm, which is called a haboob, near Mesa July 6, 2011. One of the objects appears to grow, change its shape and then glow. Some have mentioned reports that similar flashing lights and objects in the sky were observed around the time of the tsunami and earthquake in Japan.

While the sandstorm orbs appeared on CNN – there was no explanation for the saucers. Later though it is being said that the lights were actually Southwest airlines planes.

Meanwhile elsewhere in the world Fortean times reported that there was a mass grave found in Africa where the skeletal remains were not at all conventional.
A team of anthropologists found a mysterious burial in the jungle near the city of Kigali Rwanda (Central Africa). The remains belong to gigantic creatures that bear little resemblance to humans.

Head of research group believes that they could be visitors from another planet who died as a result of a catastrophe.

According to the scientists, they were buried at least 500 years ago. At first, researchers thought that they came across the remains of ancient settlements, but no signs of human life have been found nearby. The 40 communal graves had approximately 200 bodies in them, all perfectly preserved. The creatures were tall – approximately 7 feet. Their heads were disproportionately large and they had no mouth, nose or eyes. The anthropologists believe that the creatures were members of an alien landing, possibly destroyed by some terrestrial virus to which they had no immunity.

However, no traces of the landing of the spacecraft or its fragments were discovered.
I have been investigating all things paranormal for going on 17 years and I can honestly say that the paranormal seems to be set on "high" as more and more people feel that they are in the midst of something peculiar. While video after video shows up on You Tube, or on the evening news, there are people who will do their best to try and take the wind out of a sighting by dismissing it as fake.

I remember how the year started off with some remarkable UFO sightings that seemed to be similar. There were red lights in formation and another light that lowers from the red light array. These similar UFO events were recorded in Christchurch, Moscow, Chicago, Cairo, Jerusalem and Utah Then there were the UFOS that appeared over Russia and New Zealand that appeared to be blue vortices swirling and dropping red drone objects to the ground.

The UFO's over Israel were debunked even though they mimicked the same sightings all over the world. It was after this that more and more similar sightings were reported and either the online skeptics were asleep at the wheel or these cases were ignored because they weren't as hyped.

The UFO phenomenon has been one of the most intriguing topics of 2011. While Ground Zero Radio has been connected to UFO style stories, the truth is that we have increased UFO coverage because of the mountain of stories that have been reported in the first six months of 2011.

It doesn't look like it is letting up any time soon as Portland Oregon seems to be having the same UFO flap that it experienced 65 years ago in 1947. My show was interrupted days before the 4th of July with reports of UFO's, videos that were sent to document the sighting, interesting photographs and another video of a flashing red light hovering over Forest Grove Oregon.

On June 24th 1947 the word flying saucer was coined by journalists who were reporting an odd story about Kenneth Arnold who while flying his plane over Washington spotted a boomerang shaped craft that seemed to skip across the air as a "saucer would skip across water." These unknown craft were mirror bright and traveled at fast speeds, faster than any jet that would eventually show up in the skies many years later.
The "flying saucers" had arrived only because the media said so. For many years the balls of light and the strange aircraft had been seen and many theories as to what they were crept into the pulp novels of the day.

The Flying Saucer was most definitely a media creation; a marketing label developed to sell newspapers. It would become a word that not only was used to support the believers and the witnesses but it also was used in a derisive manner.

Much like the word UFO has been used to either support or taint a story about aircraft of unknown origin today. The irony is that the Military created that terminology.

The media was beginning to pay attention to "saucer hysteria" as soon as the suggestion was made. This may be the reason why we may never hear the true stories of what was really happening in an era that was just recovering from a major World War and preparing for several other smaller wars yet to come.

One of the unfortunate repercussions of media coverage of these events in 1947 was that reporters were printing stories that pigeon holed these anomalous events into the realms of pulp science fiction.

It was a clever way in which every anomaly could be conveniently classified and labeled as a "flying saucer" and eventually debunked as "Venus" or a "weather balloon." During this time, there could have been a number of significant events taking place that could very well have been glossed over or made to look like figments of an overactive imagination. That is why witness testimonies are vital to cases that over the years have become embellished or thrust into the communal mythology.

As time goes on there are a lot of people who feel that they are too sophisticated to allow themselves that a phenomenon as old as recorded history can be happening in our skies. The more you study the reports of these UFO's the more you realize that they are pretext to a global crisis.

Not only is the sighting of these craft a precursor to possible military movements, it also can be a monitor for the mental health and sanity of the consensus that fears the phantom enemy outside the confines of their control.

If there are aliens piloting these craft we have another problem entirely. All of the UFO possibilities from fakes to alien spacecraft illustrate some very interesting psychological markers that indicate an apocalyptic mind set.

The apocalyptic mind set is met with the debunking from 20th century thinkers that seem to be stuck in the past assuming that any and all sightings are being presumed extra-terrestrial when there are several facts about unconventional craft being talked about on the History channel. They forget that there are people out there that know what satellites and space stations look like, they trace sky movements, and really want a logical explanation. I would love to see a skeptic argue in 21st century thought with an open mind looking for patterns, analyzing comparative stories and footage, this way we could shed some light on what science could be behind this – instead of dismissing it as CGI, swamp gas, or weather balloons.

It would be refreshing for a skeptic to point out the use of Chinese lanterns, instead of giving us blow by blow of computer programs that can create a group of lights in formation.

There doesn't seem to be any skepticism giving us UFO information that point to terrestrial craft in use by governments. There is an only hostile attack on anyone coming forward with footage or anything that blurs across their cameras.

I want to also point out that skeptics seldom give smoking gun evidence against a non terrestrial UFO's in footage – only opinions on why they do not think the UFOS are alien in nature.

The term "flying saucer" evolved in the communal mythology to be UFO, a term that originally meant Unidentified Flying Object. But now it seems to be stuck as a marketing label on everything mysterious which includes, the Chupacabra, crop circles, mutilated cattle, Men in Black, government conspiracies, alien abductions, genetic manipulation, and everything else that seems to have no definitive answer. All of those topics have been shown to be hoaxes and yet the stories and sightings continue.

Not one skeptic can take out an entire mystery that seems to get more fascinating all over the world.

IT'S LIFE... ISN'T IT?

Back in 1997, the theory of a holographic universe was first introduced by physicist Juan Maldacena, who theorized that gravity arises from thin, vibrating strings that exist in nine dimensions of space and another of time, whereas real life exists in a universe without gravity. The comparison to the hologram is frequently made because of the way a hologram is created; it's a three-dimensional image coded onto a two-dimensional surface.

The theory suggests that the universe is built in a similar fashion, the higher dimensional part coded onto a flatter, lower dimensional part. So, on a hologram, only one part is tangible — the lower dimensional surface onto which the hologram is coded. The holographic image, though, merely looks three-dimensional. You can't, for example, touch it with your fingers. Now, pretend that's the structure of the universe.

Entertainment media has been exploring this concept for quite a while, with movies like *The Matrix* and *Vanilla Sky* becoming so prevalent in modern-day culture. The Men in Black trilogy features short segments — acting as quick, but thought-provoking jokes — that show some universe (ours or another) as being part of a much larger one. The end of the first movie, for instance, shows that our universe is the size of and held within a marble, kept in an alien's bag with other universe marbles. If we're living within a hologram and made to think it's just our normal universe, there isn't much of a way we'd know if that's how it was designed. A disturbing thought, so naturally, some very smart scientists are trying to figure out if we live in the universe as we know it — or not.

New research from scientists at the Vienna University of Technology concludes that the holographic principle is possible in the context of a mostly flat space-time continuum.

The holographic principle, simply put, is the idea that our three-dimensional reality is a projection of information stored on a distant, two-dimensional surface. Like the emblem on your credit card, the two-dimensional surface holds all the information you need to describe a three-dimensional object — in this case, our universe.

The question is if we are a hologram, who is projecting us and why? If the universe is a hologram we could be able to observe a number of unexpected mysterious glitches in our simulation reality.

After all, we can assume that not even the most sophisticated computer program is free from errors.

If we suspect that we are programmed beings living inside a simulation is there any way for us to find out if this is true?

Scientists would like to know if we really live in matrix and so, they try to test this quite bizarre concept practically. We can say that theoretically this bizarre scenario is possible. An unknown but highly advanced civilization living "somewhere" among the stars recognizes our "technologically advanced computer systems" as very primitive achievement.

These beings — having all possible technological achievements we can only imagine – want to have some fun and decide to play God.
For example, Rich Terrell, from the NASA Jet Propulsion Laboratory, California Institute of Technology has suggested that God is in fact a cosmic computer programmer.

Such advanced aliens can bring to life the universe as a simulation on a cosmic scale, with galaxies, planets and billions of stars.

Inside this so-called universe they place us, humans and give us simulated life we consider as reality.

They watch us, take notes and play us back and forth past and present to detect any and all flaws, or to eliminate any and all paradox problems. According to a recently theory proposed by Robert Lanza, author of *Biocentrism: How Life and Consciousness are the Keys to Understanding the True Nature of the Universe death might not even be real!*

We might think that we are an advanced species, but we possess limited knowledge of the world around us.

We are moved by moved by neurophysiological signals and subject to a variety of biological, psychological and sociological influences over which we have limited control and little understanding.

Physicist Alain Aspect conducted a most remarkable experiment demonstrating that the web of subatomic particles that composes our physical universe – the so-called "fabric of reality itself" — possesses what appears to be an undeniable "holographic" property.

We assume that technologically mature civilizations

Would have access to enormous amounts of computing power. So enormous, in fact, that by devoting even a tiny fraction to ancestor simulations, they would be able to implement billions of simulations, each containing as many people as have ever existed. In other words, almost all minds like yours would be simulated.

Therefore, by a very weak principle of indifference, you would have to assume that you are probably one of these simulated minds rather than one of the ones that are not simulated

Maybe this is the reason why when you boil things down to basics we as humans respond to images, numeric patterns and all language is frequency and numbers.

Science is imperfect because people are imperfect — it has always been, and so it will always be. Man's greatest paradox is the attempt by too many to interchange Magic or for the religious "God" and science replacing one with the other — when, in reality, one should lead to the other if the path is kept clear of prejudices.

With an honest pursuit of ultimate knowledge, humanity would not be facing such a cataclysm of moral and ethical problems involving science. But honesty and morality have been cast aside to embrace a substitute for "knowledge."

We are waking up to the fact that the paranormal, and beliefs in paranormal events is the new normal.

As I have reported before when quoting Robert Anton Wilson, we have created this safety net we call reality and every once in a while we are reminded that a very real existential world exists and that the spooky actions we see are all part of some quantum theory that is not easily explained.

There have been many occasions where we have been told that the universe we live in is a construct, a safe haven that we have developed to hide away from the various demons and bogey man that plague our nightmares.

I am no scientist or theologian, I have dabbled in the occult and studied all of the strangeness and peculiarities of this world and with my Fortean goggles I see the world as a playground of fascinating coincidences. I want to make this fact clear, a fact that cannot be escaped even if you are an atheist or agnostic or otherwise. There is a shared meme held by billions of people on this planet and that is the world is destined to end in some chaos.

Quantum physics gives us a new way to look at our world. If we see an object, it is because the object pops into view, if it leaves our view quickly we question if what we see was just a hallucination or if it is real and pops out of sight and out of mind.

Quantum reality gives us the ability to even question if what we saw was out of the ordinary, or plucked from another matrix to occupy this construct.

What is seen in our view is known as the field, some call it the grid. Once you take seriously that all possible universes can (or do) exist then a slippery slope opens up before you. It has long been recognized that technical alien civilizations, only a little more advanced than ourselves, will have the capability to simulate universes in which self-conscious entities can emerge and communicate with one another.

They would have computer power that differed from ours by a vast factor. Instead of merely simulating their weather or the formation of galaxies, like we do, they would be able to go further and watch the appearance of stars and planetary systems.

Then, having coupled the rules of biochemistry into their astronomical simulations they would be able to watch the evolution of life and consciousness (all sped up to occur on whatever timescale was convenient for them). Just as we watch the life cycles of fruit flies they would be able to follow the evolution of life, watch civilizations grow and communicate with each other, argue about whether there existed a Great Programmer in the Sky who created their Universe and who could intervene at will in defiance of the laws of Nature they habitually observed.

We see that once conscious observers are allowed to intervene in the universe, rather than being merely lumped into the category of 'observers' who do nothing, that we end up with a scenario in which the gods reappear in unlimited numbers in the guise of the simulators who have power of life and death over the simulated realities that they bring into being. The alien simulators determine the laws, and can change the laws, that govern their worlds.

They can engineer anthropic fine-tunings.

This may explain the various reports of alien abduction cases that we have been covering at the McMinnville UFO Festival.

Widespread publicity was generated by the Betty and Barney Hill abduction case of 1961 (again not widely known until several years afterwards), culminating in a made for television film broadcast in 1975 starring James Earl Jones and Estelle Parsons dramatizing the events. The Hill incident was probably the prototypical abduction case, and was perhaps the first where:

The beings that later became widely known as the Grays appeared (who also went on to become the most common type of extraterrestrial in abduction reports). The beings explicitly identified an extraterrestrial origin (the star Zeta Reticuli was later suspected as their point of origin). Neither the contactees nor these early abduction accounts, however, saw much attention from ufology, then still largely reluctant to consider close encounters of the third kind, where occupants of UFOs are allegedly interacted with.

In 1975, Travis Walton with six colleagues that formed a seven man wood-cutting gang sighted a 'disc-shaped object' hovering above a forest in Sitgreaves National Park, Arizona. The UFO was said to be twenty feet wide and eight foot high and dark silver in colour. With curiosity getting the better of him Travis Walton ignored the pleas of his work mates and left the car to investigate.

Travis Walton's colleagues witnessed a beam of intense blue light shoot out from the UFO and envelope Travis, flinging him back ten feet through the air. Scared and fearing that Travis Walton was now dead his colleagues drove off leaving Travis to his fate. Shortly after Travis Walton's work mates regained their nerve and decided to turn around and go back for him, but when they returned there was no longer any sign of either Travis or the UFO.

After reporting the incident the wood-cutters were suspected of the murder of Travis Walton, but each undertook and passed a polygraph (lie detector) test, the results of which suggested that either they had seen or at the least believed that they had, the UFO. Five days after his disappearance Travis Walton's brother-in-law received a phone call in which a weak sounding voice muttered "This is Travis, I'm in a phone booth at the Heber gas station, I need help, come and get me."

As is often the case with alien encounters of the Fourth Kind Travis Walton was unable to remember what had occurred during the time that he had been missing, but undergoing 'hypnotic regression' he was able to recall being taken aboard the UFO and lying in a hospital like room being monitored by three alien entities that he described as being 'large, with hairless heads and huge eyes'. It was supposedly following this that Travis later woke by the side of the highway about ten miles from where he and his colleagues originally witnessed the UFO.

There are theories about time meddlers. The time meddlers are much like the Observers in the TV show "Fringe" or the agents that appeared in the cult film The Adjustment Bureau. John Keel and UFO observer Kenneth Arnold called them "the Men in Black."

The truth is the custodians — even the alien overseers of the program can pull the plug on the simulation at any moment, intervene or distance themselves from their simulation; watch as the simulated creatures argue about whether there is a god who controls of intervenes; work miracles or impose their ethical principles upon the simulated reality. All the time they can avoid having even a twinge of conscience about hurting anyone because their toy reality isn't real, is it? They can even watch their simulated realities grow to a level of sophistication that allows them to simulate higher-order realities of their own.

Faced with these perplexities do we have any chance of winnowing fake realities from true?

What we might expect to see if we made scientific observations from within a simulated reality?

Eventually, the alien tinkering and refreshing would snowball and these realities would cease to compute. The only escape is if their creators intervene to patch up the problems one by one as they arise.

This would be the so called alien revealing – seen as an invasion and quite possibly a reboot of the system.

Let there be light.

SPACEBALLS AND OTHER JUNK

During the doom porn earthquake show last night, I had mentioned that NASA used to chide conspiracy theorists that were reporting impending doom from outer space. Back in 2012 when doomsday theorists seemed to be everywhere, from Twitter to You Tube, NASA would actually take the time to create propaganda pieces that would say, "There will be no doomsday asteroids" or "There is no Planet X" or "no UFO mother ships are passing by the ISS."

Their "nothing to see here" stance was getting tiresome and even the thought of addressing the doomsayers made me wonder what NASA was hiding. Could it be that NASA is incapable to admit that with all the activity going on above us, we are having a lot of close cosmic shaves where something the size of a house could very well crash into a populated area?

Each year, over 300 objects intersect Earth's orbital trajectory. They range in size from a soccer ball, to the size of Manhattan. It is only a matter of time, before we arrive at the wrong place at the wrong time. Some scientists believe that the Earth has the potentiality for a "kiloton equivalent" event from an in air burn up or impact about twice per year. These kiloton equivalents can happen without warning as the things we have floating above us don't often remain in the sky and come crashing down into space stations, satellites, and even populated areas.

Statistically speaking, each of us is 1,000,000 times more likely chance to die getting hit by something from space than to win the lottery.

The Pentagon confirmed that the volume of abandoned rockets, shattered satellites and missile shrapnel in the Earth's orbit is reaching a "tipping point" and there could very well be a problem where a big chunk of space junk could thrust its way through the mess, drifting gradually to hit other satellites and cause problems that could be felt for years afterward. We would see cable television stations shut down. GPS systems, phone lines, certain internet providers, weather prediction models, and perhaps even military satellites disrupted by the event.

Back in February of 2009, two satellites collided and debris was sent towards the Earth. The rain of metal was scattered over Texas and Kentucky. It also sparked a brush fire in a Texas dry field.

Back then, there was concern the debris filed that encircled the Earth could have damaged the ISS. There were also several military agencies and The Federal Emergency Management Agency on alert for any damage or harm the collision may have caused.

This week has been a banner week for UFO activity, misguided missiles and space junk. NASA of course has done their best to cut the video feeds from the International Space Station as at least three UFO's flew by it. They have also told us there will be a whole lot of space junk raining down to the Earth. Four huge spherical objects have fallen over Spain and Turkey and there will be a direct hit of space debris in the Pacific Ocean on Sunday.

Last Saturday, we all know that sky watchers in California saw what appeared to be a glowing UFO in the night sky.

Speculation started orbiting on the Internet immediately, with photos and videos trending under the hashtag, #UFO. People began calling authorities, wanting answers. Was it a ship piloted by extraterrestrials?

A celestial, cataclysmic occurrence? Was it an end time's omen?

Of course, we realized it was none of those things —just a Trident missile being tested creating more speculation over who or what the target was and whether or not World War Three is not too far away. Interesting and true to form, this Navy psy-op turned our attention away from 3 UFO's that were reportedly passing by the International Space Station.

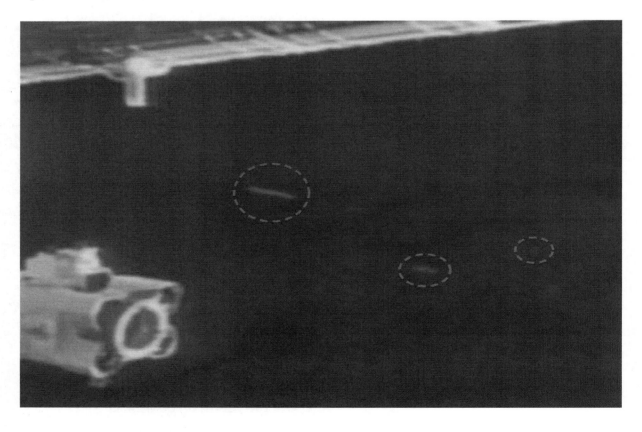

NASA cut the feed of the activities on the ISS when a donut-shaped UFO passed near the station. It was reportedly the third one this month. Footage shows a strange glowing ring floating above Earth before slowly vanishing.

When the first object passed overhead, NASA was well aware that the object was there and decided to focus on it. The light is so bright that the camera cannot focus properly.

The object also appears to be tracking the ISS, moving at a similar speed behind it.

NASA then "panics" and cuts the feed. When the footage begins again, the strange light vanishes.

There was another grainy looking UFO seen on camera that NASA dismissed as space junk. Finally, a strange doughnut-shaped UFO was spotted by NASA cameras – NASA acknowledges the UFO, zoomed in on it and cut the visual feed yet again.

There is an average of 70,000 reported UFO sightings every year, worldwide. That's an average of 192 per day. There are still many sightings that are seen by astronauts and are monitored by NASA at the International Space Station.

While much of what we see in the sky is unknown, a lot of things are simply space debris or space junk.

Most of the space junk is tracked by NASA however there are times when things fall out of the sky that make us wonder what is really up there.

In the Jim Carrey movie, The Truman Show, Truman is about to go to work when a stage light falls from the sky. Confused, he goes to check it out. The light has the word "Sirius" taped on it; a metaphor for a celestial rock falling from the sky. Truman wonders if it is some sort of space junk.

More than 500,000 pieces of debris, or "space junk," are tracked as they orbit the Earth. They all travel at speeds up to 17,500 mph, fast enough for a relatively small piece of orbital debris to damage a satellite or a spacecraft.

Usually when NASA tracks a piece of space debris that might enter earth's atmosphere, they report it to the media. However, it appears that not all space junk or even extra-terrestrial artifacts get reported by NASA.

A week ago a strange 50 lb orb was found in a remote field in the village of Calasparra in Murcia, Spain, the same day as another bizarre 50 lb round object was found at the Black Sea coastal town of Sakarya Karasu, 1,500 miles away in Turkey.

Then in the small town of Villavieja just a stone's throw from Calasparra, there were reports of another one found in a small crater last Tuesday. Now it has been reported locally that a third object was found in Spain, making four in total including the Turkish incident. The third Spanish object was discovered in Elda neighboring the region of Valencia, where a farmer found a long, metal-like object in his field and called the police.

Special agents reportedly arrived, but they deduced it posed no threat and passed it to a police station in nearby Alicante.

Authorities say that it looks as if it belonged to a space vehicle, others believe that the pieces may have fallen off of an OVNI or UFO. So far, even though there seems to be no threat, people in the areas of the crash are shaken by the incident.

Early this morning, ironically on Friday the 13th — the long-anticipated arrival of a mysterious object from outer space came when fiery debris was tracked from the United Arab Emirates.

Now, mind you no one knows what this piece of space junk broke off from. In fact, the name of the object was called WT1190F which some believe is an anagram for WTF0911.

The object had been spotted before, in 2013, by the Catalina Sky Survey at the University of Arizona. Analysis of its movements suggested it wasn't solid like rock. Rather, it had a density of about 10% that of water, according to scientists.

The encounter came just a few weeks after a newly spotted asteroid, traveling 78,000 miles an hour, zipped past Earth at a distance of about 300,000 miles. The asteroid was called the "Halloweens Asteroid" and looked like a large skull.

This raises the question as to whether or not the debris was the result of a sweeper effect where a massive celestial body near earth brings with it other rocks and junk and hurls it towards the earth.

Sweeper effects have been known to push space debris into Earth's atmosphere. There can be 300 to 400 pound pieces of space junk and rock that if they move fast enough can create several high-level dangers forcing areas to go on alert.

The obvious observation that can be made is the planet Earth is like an ocean liner that travels in a very turbulent ocean called space. Everyone knows that the oceans on Earth can be turbulent. Just think of it on a larger scale.

Intense periods of UFO sightings, falls of space debris, and unknown objects that are reported from space agencies seem to indicate that there is more to space and what is above us than meets the eye. NASA and other space agencies see these events as "small" anomalies that may or may not be part of the normal space environment. However, it doesn't take a rocket scientist to understand that many small anomalies can become not only a public relations disaster but it also increases the chances of significant problems including simultaneous failures of any space machine that runs the risk of being hit by these objects.

It also raises questions about whether or not space has become not only a space dump, but a battlefield. We recently reported in "Coloring the Wargame" that a memo submitted to congress states that "China's Naval modernization effort encompasses a broad array of space platform and weapon acquisition programs."

There is also the secret space program known as Solar Warden. This space program not only operates classified under the US Government but also under the United Nations authority.

Solar Warden is said to be made up from U.S. aerospace Black Projects contractors, but with some contributions of parts and systems by Canada. United Kingdom, Italy, Austria, Russia, and Australia. It is also said that the program is tested and operated from secret military bases located in the west desert of Utah, Area 51 and other secret locales. Many people around the world are now witnessing craft moving around in the skies and sub space that completely defy gravity. The new UFO sightings are becoming less alien and more like military platforms with collision lights.

As Peter Davenport of the National UFO reporting center once said, "There is no question that something strange is happening in the skies above us."

As a result of some recent and dramatic sighting reports, we can definitely say there is no reason to doubt he is telling the truth.

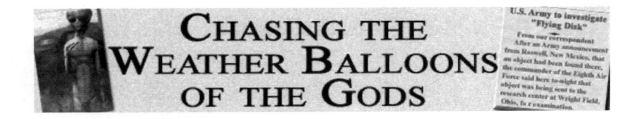

CHASING THE WEATHER BALLOONS OF THE GODS

CHASING THE WEATHER BALLOONS OF THE GODS

If you are one of the "skeptics" about the so-called Roswell incident and wish that it would go away you may not have to wait too long for that to happen. The witnesses are dying off. While the experts can speculate and render data regarding the incident, it is always best to hear what really happened from a person who was there. The story needs to be accurately told and the witnesses are vital. It is time to listen. To not reveal the truth is mockery to the memory of those who were there.

In 1945 the war in Europe was drawing to a close. It was during that period that many strange and interesting things were transpiring. Bomber crews were starting to notice glowing orbs near their planes as they flew over the German air space. The strange balls of light were displaying incredible acrobatic maneuvers and would fly at incredible speeds around the propeller driven aircraft. Some of these orbs were clocked at 17,000 to 2000 miles per hour. This was unheard of during this time.

Many of the allies determined that these orbs had hostile intent. Some planes were often forced into a dive to avoid collisions with these unknown craft. These orbs were called Foo Fighters long before the word UFO crept into the lexicon and was associated (according to the popular media) with "lone nuts" who see things in the skies, and chase weather balloons and "swamp gas."

It is a part of history that has yet to be tainted by so called "skeptics" who by name should sit on the fence and analyze yet find it good sport to try and "debunk" and make light of the documented evidence that substantiates this aerial phenomenon.

When the war ended there were questions raised as to the origin of these strange balls of light. Germany claimed that they had nothing to do with the strange lights and theorized that perhaps they were a "top secret" weapon being used by allied forces to outpace their new jet propulsion technology that was being developed.

In 1946 there seemed to be an excitement over Germany and Scandinavia regarding the sighting of fiery rockets in the sky. The Allies feared that a resurgent fanatical group of Nazis were developing rocket technologies to start another war. It was theorized that these strange new rockets were being test fired from underground bases.

People feared that they were new weapons of mass destruction and saw them moving in erratic ways shooting up into space and then coming down in fiery balls of light. Some people journeyed into the areas where they thought the "rockets" had landed thinking that perhaps there would be scorched land or even a small fire.

There was no fire to be seen. Before there were UFO's there were craft of unknown origin and they were very real. They may have even been thought of as alien to the witnesses who had never seen such aircraft before. The fascination and magic of such craft wound up in dime store comic books and science fiction magazines.

On June 24th 1947 the word flying saucer was coined by journalists who were reporting an odd story about Kenneth Arnold who while flying his plane over Washington spotted a boomerang shaped craft that seemed to skip across the air as a "saucer would skip across water." These unknown craft were mirror bright and traveled at fast speeds, faster than any jet that would eventually show up in the skies many years later.

The "flying saucers" had arrived only because the media said so. For many years the balls of light and the strange aircraft had been seen and many theories as to what they were crept into the pulp novels of the day.

The Flying Saucer was most definitely a media creation; a marketing label developed to sell newspapers. It would become a word that not only was used to support the believers and the witnesses but it also was used in a derisive manner.

Much like the word UFO has been used to either support or taint a story about aircraft of unknown origin today. The irony is that the Military created that terminology.

The media was beginning to pay attention to "saucer hysteria" as soon as the suggestion was made. This may be the reason why we may never hear the true stories of what was really happening in an era that was just recovering from a major World War and preparing for several other smaller wars yet to come.

One of the unfortunate repercussions of media coverage of these events in 1947 was that reporters were printing stories that pigeon holed these anomalous events into the realms of pulp science fiction.

It was a clever way in which every anomaly could be conveniently classified and labeled as a "flying saucer" and eventually debunked as "Venus" or a "weather balloon." During this time, there could have been a number of significant events taking place that could very well have been glossed over or made to look like figments of an overactive imagination.

That is why witness testimonies are vital to cases that over the years have become embellished or thrust into the communal mythology.

One such event that sadly has become the best example of communal mythology is the Roswell crash in 1947.

With the help of the media, and several "experts" the Roswell incident has become a fact mixed with pulp science fiction and disinformation levied by opportunists and the military combined.

That is probably the chief reason why the Roswell case is the case that most people wish would go away. Many "skeptics" and "debunkers" have come forward to say that UFO believers are chasing after the weather balloons of the gods and ignoring the real data that suggests that what crashed at Roswell was a weather balloon with crash test dummy occupants.

On June 24th 1997 The Air Force used that explanation in their response to the GAO report which concluded:

"Aliens" observed in the New Mexico desert were actually anthropomorphic test dummies that were carried aloft by U.S. Air Force high altitude balloons for scientific research.

The "unusual" military activities in the New Mexico desert were high altitude research balloon launch and recovery operations. Reports of military units that always seemed to arrive shortly after the crash of a flying saucer to retrieve the saucer and "crew," were actually accurate descriptions of Air Force personnel engaged in anthropomorphic dummy recovery operations.

The Air Force was certain that their tidy little conclusion explained why they needed hermetically sealed coffins as reported by Mortician Glen Dennis. This was why the witnesses were threatened by military personelle who warned that if any one spoke they would be picking their bones out of the desert. This is why they allegedly ordered a B-29 to fly the dummies and the weather balloon to Fort Worth and then to Wright Patterson Airforce base. The Air Force thought that it was wise to point out that many of the eyewitnesses to the events at Roswell were becoming senile and meshing many events into one solid one.

However the witnesses once again pointed out that it was the airforce that had meshed the events together, The project in which anthropomorphic dummies were used was called project "High Dive" and it was in operation in 1956. The project was not classified and the dummies were clearly marked so that if a wind carried them aloft and they were lost, civilians were offered a $25 dollar reward for their recovery.

Another problem with the report was the inclusion of pictures that purported to show space probes that easily could have been mistaken as "flying saucers." The photographs in the report were taken not in 1947, or 1957. They weren't even taken in 1967. The photos were of a Viking space probe and a NASA Voyager-Mars space probe taken in 1972! The media swallowed up the story and to this day there are many books and in depth news stories that claim that this explanation is satisfactory and that if we use Occam's Razor we will clearly see that this is "probably" the best explanation to date.

Okay.

I always hear the old Occams Razor argument when classic debunkers speak of the events that happened in July of 1947. Of course Occam's razor states that if you have two equally likely solutions to a problem, you should choose the simplest. Debunkers will tell you that the simplest solution to Roswell is that it was a weather balloon with dummies in tow. If it even comes close to the simplest explanation then why was the explanation changed three times over a 50-year period?

Occam's Razor has become a cliché "end all be all" for debunkers who think that it is an axiom of physics and a quick fix to uncomfortable or inconclusive data.

It isn't. It is obvious to me that it has become a crutch for people who just can't accept the possibility that there are things in the universe that have no explanation.

It should be pointed out that Occam's Razor does not always apply when you are dealing with cosmology or psychology, doubly so when you are dealing with parapsychology.

The simplest answer (if one still chooses to use it) is that a "craft of unknown origin crashed near the plains of St. Augustine (Roswell was the closest town and not the exact location of the crash). The Army Airforce recovered the craft. The aircraft was piloted by a human crew, which appeared to show abnormal characteristics such as a small frail body, a large head, large eyes and grayish skin color. The popular term for the craft in the news media at the time was "flying saucer" which arguably tainted the whole story and reduced it to the level of Pulp Science Fiction.

The term "flying saucer" has evolved in the communal mythology to be UFO, a term that originally meant Unidentified Flying Object. But now it seems to be stuck as a marketing label on everything mysterious which includes, the Chupacabra, crop circles, mutilated cattle, Men in Black, government conspiracies, alien abductions, genetic manipulation, and everything else that seems to have no definitive answer.

Unfortunately the Roswell incident has become a fact that has snowballed into an extraordinary myth. It was evident that when I attended the 50th Anniversary of the crash that everyone had a story to tell about the incident.

It is as if Saucer euphoria has engulfed the area and while a finite number of people were involved with the Roswell incident the number of those who claim first hand knowledge about it will go beyond the official census.

The truth is that the true witnesses are aging, dying or dead. The others can only speculate and more so, others can only believe the stories their relatives have told them. There are also countless experts who demand your belief and their stories can only carry you so far.

I am pointing this out not because I am disillusioned or disenchanted but because it needs to be said that an overreaction to the whole affair taints it and unwittingly makes witnesses look silly or delusional.

It is not far from the truth when I tell you that 50 years of Hollywood gerrymandering has made Roswell virtually unbelievable. The known facts have been embellished. A consensus history has been constructed by a small number of people who have never been to Roswell and have never talked to eyewitnesses.

If you don't believe me, the next time someone in the mainstream media writes a story that deals with UFO's or ET's count how many times the word Roswell, Area 51, and Hangar 18 come up. Also read on and see how many times Roswell and Area 51 are somehow related in the same legend. Also check out how many times alien bodies and Santilli's alien autopsy film are some how blended to show that all of them occurred in one big event.

Throw in a few crop circle legends, a cattle mutilation, and a few appearances by the Men in Black and you have a sensational news story. A story that has all of the gimmicks and trigger words that wet the appetite of what news people think the typical UFO enthusiast wants to hear.

The reality is that the new breed of UFO enthusiasts are tired of the gimmicks and want to know the truth. Roswell is not like the legend of Loch Ness, however it's edging closer to that kind of story.

For example, the main stream press will point out that Roswell is the only event that kooky UFO followers treat as something equivalent to the "Alien nativity". Many will completely overlook the events that set the stage for Roswell and the fact that Roswell was only "big news" 30 years after the alleged event.

I theorize that the reason for this is because of Hollywood and derivative movies like "Independence Day" that try and cram 50 years of information into a 2-hour popcorn film.

This does not mean however that nothing happened. There is little doubt that something fell out of the sky and that it was unknown. The authorities knew it, and official action had to be taken.

This action led to the separation of the Army and the Airforce, the creation of the CIA and President Truman signing the National Securities act which basically established a single Department of Defense.

Many skeptics claim that all testimony about Roswell is simply an overreaction to a mundane happening yet we see the actions taken by a government scrambling for answers to a complex event, an event that has been kept secret for over 50 years.

The Roswell crash scenario is a hot bed for all kinds of outrageous theory and lately it has seen the backbiting of rival theorists bashing each other and demonstrating where each story is incompatible with the other.

Article after Article and book after book can feed the mythology and create a cash cow for those believers in search of a belief, yet there are still eyewitnesses that in their final years have decided to come forward and tell it like it is.

Robert J. Shirkey was in the thick of it all in 1947 and his story is that "He was there." Indeed he was.

Shirkey is a former pilot and first lieutenant with the U.S. Army Airforce and was assisting group operations officer with the 509th bombing group at Roswell army airfield in July of 1947. Robert Shirkey was ordered by Col. Blanchard on July 8, 1947 to assemble a crew and have a B-29 ready for take-off.

Shirkey witnessed at close range boxes that were full of the debris that were loaded on to a B-29 bomber. Shirkey claims that the debris was from something extraordinary and not a weather balloon. Shirkey saw Jesse Marcel carry a box with one of the glyph covered I-beams sticking out of it.

Shirkey also recalls that a car pulled up just beneath the tail section, from which several boxes were unloaded and put in the plane.

His eyewitness accounts have made it into books and articles and now he has decided to reveal it all in his own book. It is evident after reading his book "Roswell 1947. I was there" that the United States Government and Military are lying about what really happened in the New Mexican prairie and that they have smeared the reputations of honest and dedicated men who served the country. No veteran or serviceman who fought and served our country should be treated this way.

But many have been. Such as Jesse Marcel and others. In a time where it is difficult to get an unbiased and truthful view of the Roswell affair, Shirkey's book is a breath of fresh air.

Its purpose is to bring integrity to the stories that each individual has told. He does not use trigger words or phrases that have been axioms for the stereotypical UFO enthusiast. It avoids media hype and the tantalizing mythology that has been used to create a less realistic view of what truly happened in the area of T6-R23, Chaves County, New Mexico.

He says that reporters have reported only portions of the incident and have sensationalized and falsified many things surrounding it.

Shirkey was quoted during the 50th anniversary of the Roswell incident and he remembers quite well that the "saucer" debris was loaded on to the B-29 and was flown out of Roswell. An hour later the story hit the papers:

"Suddenly we had this call from Col. Blanchard that said I want a B-29 parked in front of the Base Ops. I sent the crew down and they were ready for takeoff at about 2 o'clock. This was July 8. I came back from lunch that day and Col. Blanchard walked in behind me. He stepped back in the hallway and waved his hand at some people who were out front of the building. And they came through and down the hallway and walked out across the ramp.

They were carrying boxes of strange-looking material. One man had a piece, carrying under his arm right out in the open, about 16 by 22, coffee table sized. Maj. (Jesse) Marcel went through carrying this box with scraps of metal in it and one of the I-beams sticking up in the corner. Meanwhile a staff car had pulled up underneath the tail and they were handing some boxes up into the back door entrance."

The plane lifted off about 2 p.m., and at 3 p.m. the Roswell Daily Record hit the streets with the story of the flying saucer."

The article in the Roswell record stated:

The many rumors regarding the flying disc became a reality yesterday when the Intelligence office of the 509th Bomb Group of the Eighth Air Force, Roswell Army Air Field, was fortunate enough to gain possession of a disc through the cooperation of one of the local ranchers and the sheriff's office of Chaves County.

The flying object landed on a ranch near Roswell sometime last week. Not having phone facilities, the rancher stored the disc until such time as he was able to contact the sheriff's office, who in turn notified Maj. Jesse A. Marcel of the 509th Bomb Group Intelligence Office.

Action was immediately taken and the disc was picked up at the rancher's home. It was inspected at Roswell Army Air Field and subsequently loaned by Major Marcel to higher headquarters.

Under the direction of Colonel Blanchard the B-29 carrying the strange cargo had orders to fly to Fort Worth. They were told that the contents of the crates on board were that of a crashed plane however a destroyed plane would be sent to a salvage yard and not flown out. Shirkey arranged all of this. The important thing to mention is that Shirkey was never told to keep quiet about what he saw.

There are many questions about Roswell that seem to go unanswered by the military. While The Roswell crash has produced very little evidence of extra terrestrial origins it needs to be stated that the Military treated the wreckage and the occupants differently. All the witnesses say that it was definitely not a weather balloon.

This cargo was special and many actions by personelle need to be evaluated. Here are a few questions that need to be raised when dealing with the Roswell incident:
Why was there a need for secrecy when something as simple as a weather balloon crashed at Roswell?
If the Balloon was a Top secret spy balloon why was a picture of it splashed on the front page of newspapers around the world?
If the Balloon was used in a Top Secret Military exercise then why did a farmer have to notify them of a crash? Wouldn't something that important be tracked and if it fell to earth wouldn't it have been cleaned up and secured as soon as possible?
Jesse Marcel and others used weather balloons every day. Wouldn't they have known the difference? None of the witnesses recognized the wreckage.
If what had fallen out of the sky was a secret military aircraft wouldn't the 509th bombing group, a group used to secret activities like loading the atomic bomb be aware of that said aircraft?

The thing I find most unfortunate about Roswell is that the government is banking on the idea that after all of the witnesses have died that you will forget about what happened there. They hope that the myth making processes that tend to cloud the facts will eventually grow into a sugar coated unbelievable fairy tale.

The town of Roswell is banking on the tourism and history and continues to say that that it is a place where the aliens landed. So will the accurate stories endure? The answer is no.

History is doomed to say that Roswell was a place where a myth raged out of control about something strange that occurred in July of 1947. The truth will be taken to the graves of everyone that was affected and those who continue to chase the weather balloons of the Gods will celebrate an ever-enduring myth.

In order to understand Roswell fully is to understand the social climate of the times. It is a matter of coincidence that the Roswell crash happened where it did. It is also synchronicity that a crash took place and the rumors were that it fell from another planet. Not long after, mankind decided it was time to break the bonds of earth. To this day we still try to venture into the cosmos. To discover new worlds, and to explore the possibilities of life out there. Who knows, maybe some day we will be able to fly to a planet and crash land in one of its deserts.

I can only hope that the beings that find us are more merciful and kind than we were to them.

THE REAL IS UNREAL

It seems that as of late, we have been living vicariously through the opinion polls that for some reason are being issued for the media to gobble up and report. We first gave you the poll results on how the American people are slowly pulling out of their trance and realizing that the United States Government is indifferent to our needs and that we are finally feeling the cold neglect of our leaders.

Now, I want to let you in on a little secret and speak about an opinion poll that has me realizing that along with the various polls showing we are waking up to the malfeasance in government, we are also waking up to the fact that the paranormal, and beliefs in paranormal events is the new normal.

As I have reported before when quoting Robert Anton Wilson, we have created this safety net we call reality and every once in a while we are reminded that a very real existential world exists and that the spooky actions we see are all part of some quantum theory that is not easily explained.

A Reuter's poll of people around the world found a little more than half of the world's population believes in God and the afterlife. U.S. polls regularly show that about half of us believe they UFOs might be piloted by Almond eyed aliens from outer space.

There are plenty of people today that try to explain away the unexplainable. In fact it used to be that a good ghost story or UFO story paid off those who made the claims with book deals, movie deals and the occasional appearance on the Phil Donahue show.

Oprah is not really into UFO's and the like but just loved to push a new age religious dynamic that always makes her look far more righteous than she is. Now it seems the big money is being paid to skeptics that are really not skeptics but are highly paid debunkers and humiliators that believe that any claims of the paranormal step on the toes of true scientific method.

Many see it as good sport for those who use scientific hubris to make their point, however it is beginning to be a lot more difficult to try and explain away the unexplainable as more and more reports are being made and those that are armed with smart phone cameras are getting the last laugh.

Sure there will always be the armchair critic who will from the safety of his mothers basement troll a you tube channel reporting the paranormal, and unfortunately there will always be those who love to fool us with hoaxes but that most certainly does not mean the supernatural that is not supposed to happen, happens and with a great amount of frequency.

Believe it or not skepticism is slowly returning back to its rightful methods of open minded inquiry. Those who are now witnessing the phenomena are now doing so with respectful consideration.
This is important because before it was always a matter of rejecting the claim outright instead of investigating it and finding a logical

explanation. When one cannot be found we are left with a mystery and it is always those burning questions that motivate thought and get you to think instead of react, either positive or negative to the anomalous activity.

As the real and the unreal merge together it is becoming more of the norm for a competent investigator to welcome the disciplines of psychology, neurology and other areas of science when confronting phantoms and monsters that seem to have no logical explanation.
It is also becoming more of the norm for investigators to understand the powers and nuances of the human mind and whether or not the head is capable of projecting such experiences or if environment can create the illusion of some unexplained experience.

This does not discredit the phenomenon, it only gives us a better understanding of what we are dealing with and whether or not the zeitgeist is moving us towards better understanding of the paranormal and whether or not the fringe is really all that fringy.

It is understandable how we can all misinterpret the "normal" and "natural" as "paranormal" and "preternatural" but our fallibility in identifying such things does not completely render us as unreliable witnesses.

With the frequency of such paranormal events happening and with the advent of amateur and professional investigators to the claims of outrageous things, people are now thinking twice, about what is happening and doubting what they once doubted about the phenomena. For example, next week I will be in McMinnville Oregon for the 15th annual UFO festival. It has been called the second biggest gathering of UFO enthusiasts in the country. Of course the largest is in Roswell New Mexico in July. Both gatherings reflect on possible UFO events that took place that have been elevated to legendary status and while many will argue the impact of the Roswell incident, the McMinnville incident has never been authoritatively called a hoax or proven to be a fraudulent UFO sighting.

Paul and Evelyn Trent snapped some compelling photos on their farm just before sunset on May 11th, 1950. The negatives of the pictures were situated in the middle of the film roll. Upon inspection there were no practice photos indicating that the Trents had developed a hoax. The photos sat in the camera an entire month before they were developed at a drugstore. The photos were featured in Life Magazine in June of 1950.

To this day the UFO picture remains as unimpeachable evidence that something bizarre was in the skies that day.

Beyond the UFO stories are the stories of apparitions and ghosts. A few months ago there were many stories in the mainstream news about various hauntings of houses. One that most certainly got a lot of media attention was the haunting of Latoya Ammon's Gary Indiana home.

She still "swears by her story" of demonic possession, supernatural happenings, and unexplainable phenomena in her house. The house has since been exorcised and was recently bought by Zak Bagans who is the host of 'Ghost Adventurers'.

Exorcism traces its roots to the New Testament Gospels where Jesus frees the possessed Gadarene from a legion of demons. Recently there was a buzz in the mainstream as actress Natasha Blasick told CBS This Morning hosts Phillip Schofield and Christine Bleakley that she had been raped by a demon and that she found it to be pleasurable.

Believe it or not this phenomenon has happened enough that the condition has a name it is called spectrophilia, which is "a syndrome affecting people who derive sexual pleasure from spirits."

There have been a lot of confessions provided by nurses that provide hospice care of crisis apparitions that appear when a patient dies. Hospice nurses describe paranormal events surrounding the deaths of patients. These testimonies preclude natural explanations.

However some critics are saying that many of these stories give the impression of "universalism" where everyone in their moment of dying sees heaven. There have also been a number of TV shows and movies promoting this Idea.

One such television show is ABC's "Resurrection" which is a series about dead people who come to life. The eerie premise has captured the imaginations of viewers as the show has picked up a second season.

Some are saying that it may be the series to replace "Lost" as a supernatural mystery.

One of the less paranormal movies and more of a faith promoting film is "Heaven is For Real." Heaven Is for Real is the true story of a four-year old son of a small town Nebraska pastor who experienced heaven during emergency surgery. He talks about looking down to see the doctor operating and his dad praying in the waiting room. While the film is similar to the laundry list of stories that were provided for the movie and book "Life after Life" there are many people that see the film as a breakthrough for engendering faith in an afterlife.

Meanwhile despite the softer topics of heaven and universalist apparitions there are many stories that are now indicating that the abyss is also active and that the darkness seems to be wreaking havoc on innocent human beings in the real world.

The story of Mr. Entity is another creepy haunting account given by Deborah Moffitt who claims that the entity that haunted them from 1987 to 1991 was truly a demonic presence. His presence was first known during 1986, when paranormal activity started to occur in a house that Bill Moffitt was renting out in Rancho Cucamonga. When the Moffitt's moved away from the area later that same year, the entity followed them into their new residence.

Mr. Entity was a prescience that would write on walls and mirrors. While he would scratch satanic symbols into wood he also was an entity that new something about powerful sigils as he would leave behind a tag that looked like the alchemical triangle with a tail. A sigil that represents the triangle within the Ouroboros, made famous by German mystic Jakob Boeme.

Cris Putnam, who has been a guest several times on Ground Zero calls what is happening a "Paranormal Paradigm shift" in his new book titled "Supernatural Worldview."

Cris Putnam is saying that the Paranormal is the new normal as it has literally taken on an identity of its own as we now are bombarded with paranormal conditioning with media that now indulges in the paranormal.

The paranormal has literally penetrated our lives. It would have been unheard of 20 years ago to have a reality show where investigators hunt down and produce evidence of ghostly activity.

Close to 250, million Americans say that they believe that the paranormal is the new normal. The fringe is no longer fringe and our minds are now opening up to the esoteric world.

In a twisted way, some people are saying that these figures most certainly indicate that the majority certainly have faith in not only a heaven and a hell, but a supernatural world that is under the control of a creator.

However Putnam believes that even though it may indicate faith, it is a faith that has been misdirected. He believes that the increase of paranormal events in the world indicate that prophecy is being fulfilled regarding the apocalyptic scriptures dealing with the tribulation and the idea of Satan being released or thrown down to earth to do his profane handiwork.

Times are changing as news reports have given us brutal murders where the killers have shown superhuman strength or cannibalistic behavior. There have also been Satanic sects that openly are demanding equal time with regard to public displays of religious icons.

Recently the design of a statue of Baphomet has been revealed showing children gathered around the goat headed statue that represents Satan. The statue has been finished and is now being prepared for display on the grounds at the Oklahoma capitol.

On Monday May 12th, there will be a satanic "black mass" that is set to take place at Harvard University.

"In a recent statement, Pope Francis warned of the danger of being naive about or underestimating the power of Satan, whose evil is too often tragically present in our midst. We call upon all believers and people of good will to join us in prayer for those who are involved in this event, that they may come to appreciate the gravity of their actions, and in asking Harvard to disassociate itself from this activity."

The black mass, reenacted by members of a New York-based group known as Satanic Temple, is being hosted by the Harvard Extension Cultural Studies Club. On its web site, the club called the reenactment educational and said it is not meant to "denigrate any religion or faith." The club said a piece of bread is used in the reenactment but it won't include a "consecrated host."

At first the satanic temple had stated that they would use the consecrated host for desecration in the mass. LaVeyan Satanists do not typically perform Black Mass as a regular ritual and do not desecrate the consecrated host.

Some believe that if mass is performed grave danger may happen to Boston and the students of Harvard.

The cause and effect of such practices and the literal conditioning of paranormal activity and acceptance of the part of the paranormal that is destructive can be attributed to the strange apotheosis we have created for government and religion.

The mixture of the state and religion for the sake of state religion gives way to a more hermetic state of affairs. It is taken as a fact that the state religion will be Christianity and yet we are seeing that many of the practices of both the religious and the political are corrupt and immoral and literally set the standard for a satanic dynamic with regard to the supernatural when it should be seen as neutral.

The sympathies of the people have been and will continue to be manipulated. The paranormal activity on the planet is powerful proof that our existence has more to it than just what we experience in this dimension.

The supernatural can be made to offer us a glimpse into heaven, if we are worthy and yet we waste our supernatural world view on matters of hell and damnation.

The United States is about to be brought to ruin in a controlled paranormal demolition. Ritualistic warfare that will devalue everything that we once thought was sacred. We are seeing the beginnings of a well controlled demolition of religion and Government, only to be replaced by a leadership that is empowered by the dark forces of the underworld, possessed by the demonic and destructive dynamic.

SKUNK'D

There are many things that I have reported from my radio show that have shocked me, and anymore things don't surprise me, but to actually come right out and report that NASA has delayed the launch of their own flying saucer is amazing in many respects.

As the AP reported, " *NASA hopes to try again to launch a "flying saucer" into Earth's atmosphere to test Mars mission technology after losing the chance because of bad weather, project managers said... The space agency is working with the U.S. Navy on the Hawaiian island of Kauai to see if it can get the experimental flight off the ground in late June.*"

Once again, a saucer in the news popping up out of nowhere and the old news of a space plane X-37B and its mysterious mission confirm that there is a NASA that we see in the mainstream and a secret organization that is controlled by the military to be used as a war agency.

Not just for terrestrial wars, but for extra-terrestrial wars where a clandestine space navy is off-Earth and perhaps planning an attack from above.

One of the most vital stories to recall that prove this notion is the story of Gary McKinnon and what he revealed to the world and how he almost was jailed as an enemy combatant under the Patriot Act.

As RT reported in October 2012, *"McKinnon was arrested in March 2002 for allegedly hacking into dozens of NASA and Pentagon computers over a 13-month period from his bedroom in North London. He has admitted the security breaches but said they were unintentional and that he was looking for evidence of UFOs."*

As Michael Salla wrote in an article on ExoPolitics.org:

"McKinnon first hacked into NASA's Johnson Space Center and said he: ... found a high definition picture of a large cigar shaped object over the northern hemisphere. He said that he was so shocked by the picture that he didn't think to immediately save it. He also said that the file size was so large that is was difficult to view it on his computer. Eventually his connection was lost, and so was the picture.

When McKinnon later hacked into classified files of U.S. Space Command (incorporated into Strategic Command on October 1, 2002 soon after McKinnon was caught), he discovered a number of naval terms such as "fleet-to-fleet transfers" concerning non-terrestrial officers. He said: I found a list of officers' names ... under the heading 'Non-Terrestrial Officers'. It doesn't mean little green men. What I think it means is not Earth-based. I found a list of 'fleet-to-fleet transfers', and a list of ship names. I looked them up. They weren't US Navy ships. What I saw made me believe they have some kind of spaceship, off-planet."

He also said that the records revealed that the off-planet shuttles could hold 300 people.

In 2012, all charges were dropped against McKinnon.

Around the same time, the United States government finally declassified the OXCART program at Area 51. It seemed like a coincidence that with all of the information out of the bag, that some of what happened at Area 51 would be declassified.

Operation Oxcart was a secret operation to develop a supersonic jet that could reach speeds of Mach 3. This was eventually known as the SR-71 Blackbird project. Those who play in the world of conspiracy theory had reported this for many years before the government ever officially declassified the project.

The novelty here is that the mainstream media for many years had given the impression that this was the only program that Area 51 was involved in and that anything else "speculative" about reversed alien technology can be put to rest. New ideas are now emerging about what cover stories, and disinformation about UFO's and aliens to cover up covert testing of special craft that were used for our protection in the paranoid era of the cold war.

What we are getting are table scraps from a project that was well known for years. Not that the scraps aren't satisfying, they just create an even bigger appetite for more information, we get the bones and wait for raw meat. Area 51 is a huge onion with layer upon layer that will be revealed when it is necessary. OXCART is finally becoming an official program and the details are being well controlled and all other speculation or books released before the official declassification can all be discounted now right?

Not quite.

Modern flying saucer mysteries were often sold alongside dime store pulp science fiction magazines back in 1950's and interest was limited to what was on the Hollywood screen invading small town USA. Much of what we know about flying saucers and UFO's has been hijacked by the media. Even from the beginning when Kenneth Arnold first reported his sighting the media took what was a sighting of flying wedges to flying saucers. Eventually the media corrected it with the term 'UFO' and from 'UFO' the definition somehow stuck as an alien space craft even though most logical ufologists were well aware that secret military operations were creating aircraft that had basically the same aerodynamics as those so called mythological flying saucers.

The Cold War would breed a lot of paranoia and no one questioned authority. If superiors spun tales of aliens and UFO's we can thank the Cold War intelligence ops for contributing to the mass hysteria. We can also conclude that from the new information that there seems to be a need to confuse people about aliens, space weapons, exotic flying craft and other such mechanized death because when people are fed confusing information they just stop caring about the subject matter.

If you look at the Roswell story you still get three or four ridiculous explanations for the event and a gullible media that still cynically debunks anyone who doesn't buy into their 'weather balloons of the gods' theories.

Nobody has confessed to the public that anything that happened at Roswell or Area 51 had anything to do with weather balloons. Facts are simple, we were working with Nazi scientists that surrendered at the end of World War II to produce rockets and supersonic plane technology that was abandoned at war's end. All of the technology was allegedly given to the scientists form alleged beings channeled by supernatural means.

In the Sudetenland's Owl Mountains near the Polish/Czech border many scientists who were committed to the great Secret of the Black Sun worked in underground facilities buried in the Wenceslaus mine. They hired slave labor to carry out experiments with super weapons. Hitler required round the clock work on what he called kriegsentscheidend. A term meaning "make-or-break factor." The weapons that were being made were actually some of the most remarkable doomsday devices ever conceived. Hitler wanted so badly to be victorious in the war he pushed for Der Wunderwaffen or "Wonder Weapons."

As Wikipedia notes, the SS *"supposedly developed by 1939 a revolutionary electro-magnetic-gravitic engine which improved Hans Coler's free energy machine into an energy Konverter coupled to a Van De*

Graaf band generator and Marconi vortex dynamo (a spherical tank of mercury) to create powerful rotating electromagnetic fields that affected gravity and reduced mass."

Don Phillipson's 2005 article about the Nazi bell device says, *"Reportedly the project was considered by the Nazis as of such importance that it was security classified as "War decisive", as important as their research to develop an atomic bomb."*

As Peter Crawford explains in his 2011 post on the 'Occult History of the Third Reich':

"Skeptics always say that if the Nazi saucers existed, and they were such a secret and effective weapon, why weren't they used to insure the victory of the Third Reich?

The simple truth lies in the fact that these machines, despite their superior overall performance to conventional piston-engine aircraft and early jets, could not be realistically adapted to any useful military role other than the most basic transport and recon work.

The ships did fly, and there is plenty of evidence to support that the technology and science was not limited to just disc work.

There were other modifications being done to the Vril saucers.

There is also evidence to support that test flights were done over Europe and the United States."

Most of these aircraft and the secrets that came with them were introduced into the private sector and it can be concluded that various aerospace companies, many in the Northwest were busy back engineering these exotic craft as well.

As the Alliance for Human Research Protection notes in their 2010 article, 'Legacy of Nazis in America': *"the Justice Department finally released a report by the Office of Special Investigations about the secret safe haven US officials gave Nazi criminal scientists–in direct defiance of President Harry Truman's policy."*

The DOJ report says, "*Many of the 1,600 scientific and research specialists and their dependents brought to America under Project Paperclip had been deeply involved in Nazi society during the war.*"

Many of the researchers worked in aerospace technology fields. Many were relocated to Fort Bliss in Texas, Dayton, Ohio and White Sands Proving Grounds in New Mexico.

Nazis in former positions of intelligence gathering were part of a group called 'the Org'. The group operated not as an American entity, but as a group set apart from American OSS intelligence operations. They would work for us until a sovereign German government could be established.

This meant that they worked for the U.S. as card carrying Nazis and fueled Cold War intelligence. Nazis were also given jobs in American aviation while Americans were being laid off.

Nazi aviation engineers were hired at Boeing, Lockheed, Martin Marietta, North American Aviation, and other airplane companies. There are some reports that a few of the Nazi scientists worked for aviation and blimp companies in the Northwest.

The aerospace scientists not only revealed to the United States the secret German saucer technology, but designs for the Luftwaffe flying wing or wedge designs that evaded radar detection.

They learned that Hermann Goring secretly funded the flying wing projects along with other well-known Americans and their companies. General Motors, Ford and General Electric were important in providing machines for the Nazi war effort. Henry Ford had a role in Germany's prewar Nazi military buildup.

U.S. Army Intelligence reported that the 'real purpose' of the truck assembly plant that opened in Berlin in 1938 was to produce "'troop transport-type vehicles" for the Wehrmacht. Another contributor to the Nazi Luftwaffe aerospace projects during World War II was Prescott Bush, the father and grandfather of two American Presidents.
In 1947 Wernher Von Braun a commissioned SS Officer and member of the Nazi party worked on the US Army intermediate range ballistic

missile program until he and several of his other Nazi Colleagues were assimilated through Project paper clip into NASA. Von Braun worked at White Sands New Mexico and also worked with the Navy at Wright Patterson Army Air Force Base in Dayton, Ohio. Von Braun also worked in Huntsville, Alabama.

Of course, the tests were also done at Area 51. Others were done at White Sands New Mexico. The Cold War was beginning and both the soviets and the United States were using Nazi scientists to develop more nuclear armaments all pointed at each other. One false move and the button would have been pushed killing untold millions of Russians and Americans.

Isn't it a coincidence that both Area 51 and the Nevada test site were in the same area? Isn't it a coincidence that after the 1943 move to bring Nazi scientists to America to work in Northwest aviation companies the first UFO sightings of the 1940's were reported in the Puget Sound area of Washington state?

Isn't it also further coincidence that the Maury Island incident and the Kenneth Arnold sightings all happened within weeks of each other in Washington state – and then one week later a so-called saucer crash landed at Roswell, New Mexico?

Intelligence and histories that were once top secret are becoming well known. The Nazis were reverse engineering aircraft that were allegedly inspired by extra-terrestrials and powerful secret societies. The same activities were being done after the war in secret facilities like Area 51. The Cold War veterans were probably never told of the secret histories of new technology. They just toiled away keeping us safe.

As many projects are being declassified there are a number of people that have literally blown the whistle on how these new aircraft were modified and back engineered from both Nazi and so-called extra-terrestrial designs.

It has been rumored that the Area 51/ S–4 facilities at Dugway Proving Grounds in the West Deserts in Utah have been working feverishly on aircraft that can be used for surveillance and for the delivery of scalar weaponry. Both have also shown interest in the delivery of biochemical agents through the use of stealth aircraft and direct space travel to platforms in space that are capable of launching space planes capable of reaching the Moon or Mars.

A number of whistleblowers have now emerged revealing how corporate involvements with black budgets have been achieved. With the advent of "disclosure" and "declassification", non-military corporate whistleblowers have come forward with hidden information about they have seen.

Again, Michael Salla has reported that a *"deceased corporate whistleblower revealed how during the mid-1980s, he worked for six months as an archivist for a large aerospace defense contractor based in California. It was a temporary assignment with his employer at an obscure office building. The archivist found many files dealing with flying saucers and extraterrestrial life. The files contained: "Reports, photos, media materials (tapes, films, video cassettes) and material from crashed saucers." When asked where the files came from he revealed the "materials came from everywhere. CIA, Air Force, Navy, Army, DARPA, NORAD, DoD, FBI, and government officials to name most."*

Ben Rich, former CEO of Lockheed Martin Skunkworks, says that many of the classified UFO and alien secrets have been moved from secret 'X-Files' in the government and military to corporate aerospace companies and are protected under corporate secrets laws. This means that even with the freedom of Information act you can come up empty handed about possible reversed engineering, aliens, and any missions into space that are not officially recognized.

Ben Rich again adds that,*"There are two types of UFOs — the ones we build, and ones THEY build. We learned from both crash retrievals and actual "Hand-me-downs." The Government knew, and until 1969 took an active hand in the administration of that information. After a 1969 Nixon "Purge", administration was handled by an international board of directors in the private sector."*

Former astronaut, Dr Edgar Mitchell recently confirmed an incident in 1997 where the Head of Intelligence for the Joint Chiefs of Staff was supplied the code names of UFO related off-Earth projects, but was denied need-to-know access. According to the book MILABS there has been recorded cases of abductions where both Military and "reptilian" aliens have been present. Some UFO abductees have reported that they have also been kidnapped by military intelligence personnel (MILAB) and taken to hospitals and/or military facilities, some of which are described as being underground and others out in space.

Now it seems that some of the secrets we have heard about in the past are now showing themselves in mainstream reports and some people with their eyes to the skies have snapped pictures of stunning delta shaped or triangular shaped craft that like in Kenneth Arnold's day *"skipped across the air like a saucer on the water."*

It's like we are beginning to see a renaissance of UFO activity and all the fun can be in trying to figure out just what are the ones we have built and the one's THEY have built.

ARIEL SCHOOL: FOR THE CHILDREN

When I get into the paranormal mindset and I initiate discussions about the possibility of not being alone in the universe, it can be met with criticism by those so caught up into their politics that they cannot or will not listen to anything but political talk that confirms what they already knew.

I know that for weeks I have been talking about corrupt politics and have faced the ridicule of people who feel too comfortable with the idea that their government would not betray them. However, throughout history, even before anyone heard of Barack Obama we knew that the political sphere of influence was a corrupt one.

Government has a tendency to abuse its power, and it tends to downplay the transcendence of people and their ability to outgrow certain myths that have been spun about leadership. However there are other myths that we always fall back on because somewhere in the mythos we know that there must be some darker power in control. That this power has been unleashed in some form like a disease and that there seems to be a "programmed" response to this power that remains as pervasive as it ever was.

That "programmed" response is quite simply inertia. There seems to be no real response from people. It is as if we have turned to stone, like a deer in the headlights unable to respond as we are being toyed with, hijacked, and spiritually exhausted by vampiric beings that use us as resources that can be easily removed when we are no longer of use to them.

For those who want to hear how miserable and alien our government is, I can assure you that it will always be that way. The reason may be as simple as admitting that there has been a silent take over and that for many years we have been groomed to accept this type of alien behavior from our leaders.

We may even go as to far as to say that they have been compromised by a power so dark and so foreign to our way of life that we can only hypothetically say that our leaders are merely shells being controlled by spiritual entities that have invaded their minds and control their movements.

The thoughts of interaction between leaders and entities can be an intense and stunning hypothesis, however it is not really new to assume such possibilities.

In various commentaries and studies of biblical or primitive cultures, I have been looking for patterns in belief systems that go back many millennia, and have uncovered what seems an inescapable truth.

This truth is that this planet has a rich history of cataclysm and rebirth, and that mankind has earned its right to evolutionary supremacy. However, that supremacy is temporary, predicated upon an agreement of mutual permission between mankind and an order of godlike beings that go by several names.

Zecharia Sitchin has written about the ancient "gods" and has produced evidence that purports to demonstrate that the ancient gods of Sumer were truly space-faring aliens.

While Sumer and the surrounding lands of the Middle East are the theater for the wars of today, in the past Hitler and the Nazis believed that the people who lived in this area of the world were the true descendants of the gods. The Nazis believed that they had the knowledge of the secret rulers.

In their quest to find the alien connection, millions of people were murdered. There was the occasional story that claimed that Hitler himself had been haunted by visions of alien entities demanding that more had to be killed.

The knowledge of these beings has been suppressed and the churches have corrupted the histories and accounts of these entities. Religion has covered up the various stories that conclude that we are not alone in this universe and that we are at the mercy of beings that have no bias or regard for what we may consider to be morality.

The histories of these entities and their character have been manipulated. We are told that we are supposed to love them or they will arrive with wrath to slay those who do not obey their whim.
History is determined by the bias of the dominant hierarchy.

There is also the warning from these entities that we have been charged with the responsibility of protecting progeny, to be stewards of the planet and protect its environment in order to sustain resources. These messages have been part of the alien UFO lore for more than 50 years and now they are becoming part of the zeitgeist as environmental concerns are now a matter of politics and that children become collateral damage in policies that bankrupt the future and leave them barren of resources.

"In 1994, teachers and school officials at the Ariel School in Ruwa, Zimbabwe were astonished when no less than 62 students claimed to have had a bizarre and terrifyingly prophetic encounter with a UFO and its unearthly occupants."

The children witnessed 2 small occupants who impressed upon them through telepathy that 'we are not properly looking after the earth, or the area'. The children also felt extreme fear regarding these beings that they classified as alien.

I remember watching a documentary on the subject and I was fascinated with the children's sincerity and the look on their faces.

The children all agreed that the occupants of the craft were about one meter or 3 feet tall, with slender necks, long black hair, and very large eyes.

They walked down the craft, and proceeded in the direction of the children.

When one of the entities noticed the children, he disappeared, and was next seen in the back of the UFO. Within moments, the craft took off, vanishing into the sky over the school.

Many of the children were understandably frightened, the little man had evoked many stories they had heard about demons and ghosts. In fact there were a few children who told investigators that the entities may have been be demons known as the Tokoloshi, which are believed to be eaters of small children.

Some of the children ran to the mother who was attending the snack bar, but she did not believe their story, and continued with her duties. *"Two of Ufology's most respected investigators researched the Ariel School sighting. Cynthia Hind, now deceased, was known as Africa's top notch researcher, and she was at the school the next day."*

"She requested the school's headmaster, Colin Mackie, to ask the children to make drawings of what they had seen the day before. When Hind arrived at the school, there were some 35 various drawings and sketches waiting for her."

"Most of the drawings were very similar in their depictions of the craft and being."

The drawings showed pictures of a UFO which landed in a field and a dark being with large black eyes. The headmaster of the school told Cynthia Hind that he felt that the children were telling the truth about what they had seen.

One of the students, a young girl, told Hind, "I swear by every hair on my head and the whole Bible that I am telling the truth."

Child after child was interviewed alone or in groups. Many of the children were able to share drawn pictures of a saucer like object that had round windows running along the side. The so called entity or alien wore a black and shiny suit and what was rare is that the entity had long black hair.

"Most descriptions of aliens usually portray the typical slender look with large black eyes but black hair is quite uncommon. The older students said that they felt that the creatures communicated with them somehow, sending the message that we humans are destroying our planet, polluting the environment in ways that will have dire consequences."

The students claimed that the planet was to go through abrupt changes when they were to become adults and that it is important for them to be prepared for these changes.

"The event began at approximately 10:15 am. while the children — who ranged in age from 5 to 12 years old and were of African, Asiatic and European descent — were playing in the field adjacent to the school during their mid-morning break on the already scorching, 91° day."

"The children claimed that while they were playing they noticed three "silver balls" soaring in the sky above the school. These orbs, which quickly caught the attention of the whole group, intermittently flashed red and would disappear in a burst of light and then reappeared in another section of the sky."

"Although the area where the UFO had landed was forbidden to the children due to proliferation of thorn bushes, poisonous snakes and spiders it was not fenced off from the schoolyard." This allowed the

frightened children to approach the unusual object and somehow receive communication from the entities.

"The teachers at the school later admitted that the sixty-two children were essentially unsupervised while in the schoolyard during morning recess and claimed that they ignored the student's fearful cries."

One teacher noted that they were in a faculty meeting and assumed that the children were merely playing and that what they were hearing was normal schoolyard sounds.

The children claimed that the aliens put into their heads apocalyptic images of the future and that they felt that it was a warning that the planet was about to be destroyed or the world was ending.

The event happened for about 15 minutes and soon the beings along with their glowing space ship had vanished.

Just two days prior to the event, *"over 100 children at the Pier House School which is located 25 miles from Rawa, watched as a UFO hovered and apparently searched for a place to land. At the same time the school kids at Pier House were awed by these celestial antics, all of the school buses in the Ruwa school district apparently lost the use of their radios, receiving nothing but static."*

The late Dr. John Mack was one of the psychologists that was called in to speak with the children. In his investigation he found that the twelve children he interviewed gave consistent and reliable accounts of the occurrence, leading him to believe it was not a case of mass hysteria, but a genuine alien encounter.

"While the lack of adult witnesses has led some to conclude that this incident is nothing more than a prank produced in the fertile minds of children, one must consider if it is remotely feasible for 62 pre-teens to concoct a successful hoax that requires the youngest of the bunch to feign terror while the eldest jeopardize their reputations by claiming to not only have seen an alien, but to have shared a psychic connection with it."

"Not to mention the sheer psychological effort it would take to corroborate a tale as elaborate as this. It should also be noted that in the 19 years following this harrowing event, there have been no public claims that this was a hoax made by the eyewitnesses, some of whom are now parents themselves."

Once again as a point of reference, I look at the book "Childhood's End" and realize that the irony of the aliens is that no matter how advanced they are, they envy the lives of humans. The Overlords find a way to have the children join the Overmind and in the process set out to destroy the earth in order to establish the new utopia.

The alien mission is to teach the children the secrets of the universe, to warn them of impending environmental disaster. The children begin to develop their new powers of being able to communicate telepathically and to utilize what has been called remote viewing. This is where they see the images play into their heads of a virtual apocalypse that the aliens see as beneficial; however, it turns into a self-fulfilling prophecy.

Can the programming that was revealed at Ariel be part of the alien mission which is to plant the vision of self destruction in our minds? Can this be the agenda of any organized agreed upon prophecy?

The way in which the children of these dispensational generations are incorporated into the so called alien programming is similar to of Christian descriptions of prophetic visions that are given through angels and lights and other such anomalies that we read about in the ancient texts.

And as Jesus Christ pointed out, the meek are the inheritors of Earth and that children are an intricate part in the kingdom of God. The establishment of the new paradise is predicated upon the progeny and how they are taught and in the case of this alien encounter "programmed."

Perhaps, as we move closer to an alien disclosure and that scientific and technological miracles will leave us with artificial spirituality, we are compelled to put constraints on how far a symbolic or allegorical comparison between guardian angels, angels, demons and aliens should be made.

It seems that it is inevitable that these attitudes will change over time. They must change upon a direct knowledge and revelation of the method.

In most religious circles, the change in thought or comparison will be met with cynicism and this is why we are challenged to be as children when we learn of these so-called secrets of the universe.

THE NEW AND EVERLASTING EDEN

In the Book "Gods of Eden," William Bramley accidentally uncovered a sinister connection between UFO's and major disasters. As a lawyer and war historian Bramley had set out to write a book about war and during his studies he was finding that before cataclysmic events or major wars reports of anomalous activities in the skies above the earth takes place.

Bramley has documented that UFO's and alien appearances are subtle and not overt attacks on mankind. They appear before during and after a major disaster or cataclysm to observe. Bramley contends that governments and the major religions know this but do not know their intent and that is why it is difficult to disclose the real mission of these beings.

Many still cling on to points of view that dismiss outright the very notion of extra-terrestrial intervention and yet they embrace the idea of an extra-terrestrial God being in control. Lately I have been noticing a pattern in catastrophic events and the appearance of extra terrestrial anomalies before during and after these events.

If you recall at the first of the year there was a UFO flap where UFO's were seen over the west Desert of Utah. Three red lights were seen in formation over the desert. A white shimmering light was then lowered to the ground. There were many witnesses who saw this event take place.

The entire event was seen over a secret Military installation. Hours later the same UFO was seen over Israel, hovering over the dome of the rock. Even though there were three of four different views including and observatory recording the data on this sighting, the internet was quick to dismiss the story as fake, Even though coincidentally there was a huge uprising of the Muslim brother hood in the Middle East just after the sighting.

I contend that the sightings were real, because no one who discussed any of the debunking addressed the Utah sighting. It should have been considered in the data and the locations of both should have been considered. When you have UFO activity over a well known Military installation and another over a holy shrine, it is important to take notice and to be just as cautious in debunking as well as accepting the recording of the document outright, especially during a time of war.

Some of the world's darkest events have been linked to an alien presence on earth.

It can be said that many of these darkest times have spawned new religions and these religions have been spawned form celestial events. Saul saw a bright light and changed his name to Paul and became an evangelical Roman.

Even Mohammed was visited by an entity in a cave and he even questioned whether or not he had come in content with a Djinn. He then assumed that he had come in contact with the angel Gabriel. Joseph

Smith the 14 year old Mormon prophet claimed that he too experienced something that can only be described as similar as an alien experience with beings claiming to be deity directing and guiding him with the organization of a church.

There is also the question of a forged document that the church tried to suppress that mentions that one of the entities that visited Joseph smith looked like a white salamander. A white salamander would look or even mimic the look of what we now see as an alien gray. However the document that was presented to the church by Mark Hoffman turned out to be a forgery, but was considered at the Time By Gordon B. Hinckley knowing full well that information such as this could have been created by enemies of the church to discredit the faith and perhaps make it out too look like an alien or sorcerers cult.

Truth is most religions are alien cults. Most secret societies stem from secret information that had been imparted to man from the gods.
In paradise we read that Adam and Eve, a metaphoric representation of mankind found an interesting relationship with the serpent, another metaphor for a being that obviously is an alien or some sort of intelligent operative that creates chaos.

The demons or serpent beings described by biblical texts and ancient scrolls of Nag Hammadi are simply put, agents of chaos that act without thinking of consequence. They conduct their activities for the betterment of evolution regardless if we as humans assess it as good or evil.

The interpretations of paradise seldom point out that some of the inhabitants of the biblical Eden were in fact upright walking "shiny" creatures that had a grayish copper color. They were known as the Nachash an upright creature that did not speak but spoke to the mind or whispered to the mind on mankind knowledge.

It is written in many biblical commentaries that the Nachash had the ability to possess the souls of man and force them into doing things against their will. Many were taken away and brought back with the inability to speak. Others were found on alters as sacrifices to the Gods. This is where many believe the stories of Cain, Abel, Abraham and Isaac came from. Tradition has always been that the Gods, the shiny beings, all demand blood sacrifice in order to be appeased.

The Pre-Adamic civilizations are the very civilizations that are rich in the stories of vampiric gods or beings that have come down from heaven to devour mankind. This is often overlooked by new age believers in divine alien intervention.

It is beginning to appear as if there is some sick cooperation between mankind and darker alien forces that create a cloud of death and chaos in order to control human beings on this planet.

With our egos in check we must understand that while we believe that we are well advanced and educated, the reality is pointing to the idea that the ancients before us had all kinds of relationships with beings that lived outside of the earth and that they often fought for their own safety as the beings from the skies often wanted women, children and blood offerings for sustenance.

It may be hard to believe but much of what has been covered up by religions and governments regarding our affairs with these entities are actually well known by those who are members of so called secret societies. We see these scenarios played out today just like they were anciently.

The core intelligence that accompanies aliens is that they are actually harbingers of doomsday activity and when they are seen in greater numbers we tend to see disaster late. It is almost as if the watchers are here to see pivotal moments in history.

On September 6th, 2001, 3 days prior to the September 11th 2001 attacks there was a major UFO sighting over Carteret New Jersey. Unidentified objects appeared as lights in a huge V-type formation moving silently through the air over the Arthur Kill Waterway (just South of Newark International Airport). The event was witnessed by hundreds of onlookers, including police officers and a church reverend, the sighting was reported the next day by every major news organization. People that had experienced the sighting actually felt that it was similar to a religious experience.

The events that followed the UFO sighting, namely the attcks on the United states has also been considered to be akin to a religious event. Many still cling on to points of view that dismiss outright the very notion of extra-terrestrial intervention and yet they embrace the idea of an extra-terrestrial God being in control.

It is becoming more evident that the UFO Intervention has its drawbacks and the histories of their entanglements with humans should be considered when attempting to disclose their existence.

You may see the future unfold with a whole new heaven and earth, a new order promising you the new and everlasting Eden.

CORPUS DELICTI

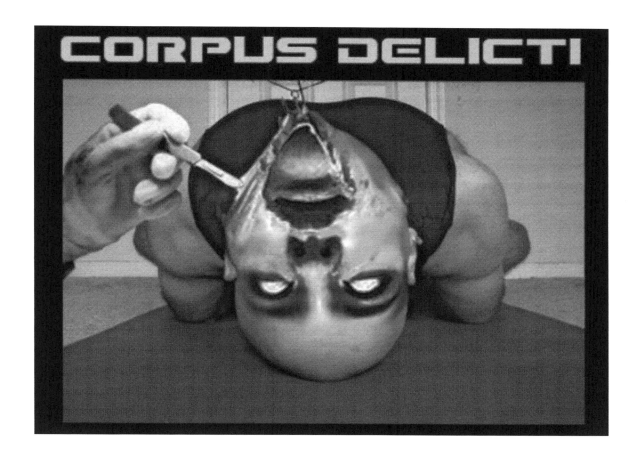

CORPUS DELICTI

As the sun sets and the night falls earlier, tales seem to spin about visitations by human-hybrid looking beings. Things that go bump in the night always bump louder when they are hovering over your bed at night beckoning you to come with them. Whether they offer you eternal life with the elixir of blood or beg you to go with them in their ship of light, the visitor phenomenon has been quieted down with the passing of one of the top most researchers, Bud Hopkins. Hopkins had recorded countless entity abductions and as he got on in years had said that these entities had the power to shape shift into human form. However during a Ground Zero show I confronted him about shape shifters and asked about the Djinn, and the half man reptile entities cited by others like David Icke.

He told me that he would never go there and that these beings are Satanic. I tried to get him to elaborate on the satanic nature of abduction, and he couldn't continue, he excused himself gave me an excuse for leaving and then he hung up the phone. He wrote me and told me that the vampire, satanic side of aliens didn't exist and that these were demonic experiences and not in his realm of expertise. It is what is inside of you, your belief system that dictates how these beings appear to you.

Now that he has died, I am now facing n an entity investigation of my own.

Reptilian aliens or demonic entities are said to be back on the Coast of Oregon and now I am beginning to see that perhaps this was all foretold. Maybe Bud Hopkins knew and it is unfortunate that he is gone.

There have been others who have stated that the reptilian groups have already landed on earth and that they organized a colony in the pacific. They have move in among us and in some cases have been part of the experiments that have been carried out on humans. Many humans have been subjected to brutal mutilations and have disappeared, while others have been safely placed back in their beds and left with the traumatic memory of being corralled and having their blood taken, their reproductive organs analyzed and having sperm and ovum removed for hybridization purposes.

There have been others that were not so lucky.

In 1994 an abduction case was reported in Brazil and after the report a body was found brutally mutilated and exsanguinated. The male was subject to a brutal systematic mutilation. Authorities had no clue who or what was responsible. The culprits were specific about what body parts they wanted.

They removed the left eye, the left ear, the lips, the tongue, and the jaw bone. In the upper torso, two "drainage holes" were perfectly cut into the chest.

And the entire rectum track had been cored out leaving a large gaping hole, similar to how an apple core remover will slice out the center leaving the outside fully intact.

This case has been regarded a mystery and there are many people who are suspecting and alien abduction and mutilation. Exact body parts taken, blood also taken and areas of the body removed just like in most cases of animal mutilation.

The autopsy report would reveal more about what happened than what the police could produce. The autopsy report states: "We observed the removal of the right and left orbital areas, emptying of the mouth cavity, pharynx, oropharynx, neck, right and left armpit area, abdomen, pelvic cavity, right and left groin area."

Precise "cookie cutter" holes were discovered in strategically positioned throughout the body used for extracting internal organs. This level of precision suggests that the operation was executed with speed, the application of heat or lasers, all occurring as the subject was still alive.

The autopsy conclusion implies that the victim died of a heart-attack due to extreme pain. This means that the victim was almost certainly alive while the mutilation took place.

If this is a case of alien mutilation, then perhaps we need to reevaluate the purpose and so called mission of these alien beings that visit the earth.

I have been investigating recent reports of alien activity, missing persons, and demonic reptilian appearances along the coast and while there have been a few calls to the show confirming all suspicion that something strange is going on – A recent message I received from a listener indicated in 2007 that there was a case of human mutilation similar to what happened in Brazil. A body was found by hikers, about 20 miles northwest of Forest Grove, near Brown's camp. The body was burned, disemboweled and dismembered. The eyes had been surgically removed and that both arms had been severed at the elbow.

Autopsy revealed that it was a white or Hispanic male in his 30's. No one knew how long the body had been at that location. There have ben a number of people who lived in the Warrenton area, Astoria, Seaside, Wheeler, and Nehalem bay who have claimed that something strange has been happening at the coast. Anything from UFO's to abductions, missing persons, vampires and cults. The entire area seems to be a paranormal hotspot.

In the pilot episode of Chris Carter's successful TV series the X-files a strange tale is told about Vampire alien entities abducting young people and leaving their bodies behind with two cookie cutter type holes in their backs.

The tale begins with a young woman dressed only in a nightgown stumbling through a darkened forest at night. She falls into a small clearing and sees an immense light growing over a nearby hill. As the leaves surrounding her swirl up in a circle around her, a figure approaches from the light and enters into the swirling Vortex. The figure stands over her as the light engulfs them both.

The encounter and the deaths of several young people in a small Oregon town near the Coast are investigated by Fox Mulder and Dana Scully. Mulder is convinced that vampiric aliens are responsible for abductions and the brutal bloodletting. What they had discovered is that there were three other deaths in the area and that three different examiners had signed off on the death reports that nothing unusual was seen in the autopsy,

Allegedly the case that Carter presented in the original episode of the X-files is based on some truth. It is a truth that has been covered up by authorities about the Oregon coast from south to the Northern most areas near Washington has been cited on numerous occasions to be a hot bed of alien abduction activity and that the X-files case was based on numerous reports of missing persons from Bray's Point to Wheeler and Warrenton.

Stanley Arthur Fulham, a UFO researcher who died in December of 2010 had an interest in the activity happening along the Oregon coast. He had remarked that there have been reports in the past of strange maelstroms that form in the wooded areas up the coast. The whirlwinds are reported to be warm with red blue and white light that ease the mind and then whisk you away.

The idea of alien abduction in the area is the hardest thing that residents can wrap their head around. Yet, there were many documents released from the FB I and even England's department of defense that were once classified revealing that the Oregon Coast seems to have a great number of missing person reports during increased sightings of strange lights and unexplained portal openings.

The view that any increase in the number of aliens taking people while in their beds – based on local police and media reports – includes evidence that is sketchy at best. To even suggest such an event, alien or even cult sacrifice is met with all kinds of derision and yet there are so many people that wind up missing and police admit "there's no real way to know where they are."

Fulham did claim before he died that the truth about these events would be revealed in 2011. He claimed that activity there would increase and that there would be no doubt that alien visitors would arrive. Their light ships would be seen all along the Pacific coast.

Fulham is most famous in UFO circles for co-authoring the book "Challenges of Change" that predicts UFO contacts and increased sightings in the year "2011."

He claimed that increased solar activity will reveal that the "watchers" are above us and the strange electromagnetic changed will create an atmosphere similar to the mass UFO sightings in Mexico, July 11, 1999. The British UFO files and also several leaked sources from Julian Assange of Wikileaks actually mentions the Oregon Coast as a place of odd activity, UFO sightings, abductions and Cult ritualism involving human sacrifice.

The Oregon coast has long been associated with UFO encounters due to such things as the geologic oddity of rock formations along the coast that some say are markers for UFO visits. In fact, Stonefield is perhaps the most secluded and exclusive of the central Oregon coast parks. There are formally declassified documents at a nearby Newport historic museum points to a period during World War II and then in the late 1950's when "the U.S. government installed numerous secret look out facilities in the area around Cape Perpetua."

What's interesting to local UFO hunters is that one of these "stone" lookout bunkers still sits near the top of Cape Perpetua that looks right down on Stonefield Beach.

The area if the coast seems to be a magnet fro such activity, because it has been speculated that the bloodlines that came from the area have ties to the Illuminated watcher's that are allegedly part reptile part human, What is interesting is that in a lot of alien, demonic possession cases exorcists and investigators have said that those who have been tormented by such entities have been chosen because of their genetics. In most cases, line of contact and the gradually building assault can be traced back to childhood. It could be said, in general, that the process of possession has already begun before either the target or those around him are aware of the signs. In most cases there is a sensation of the presence before an actual encounter takes place.

I reported about an attempted alien abduction near Coffenbury Lake in Oregon where the male witness claimed that his female partner warned him that he would see a blinding red light prior to his attempted abduction. The woman sensed the presence at the same time as the dog and later the man was caught in a vortex and red and white light feeling as if his body was superheated. The woman claimed she was watching him disappear.

Whatever is happening on the coast of Oregon is the most fascinating mystery I have ever reported. It tops the Skinwalker investigations of Utah and the UFO fallen angel reports in Davis California. This case is still open and the witnesses need to speak, Could there be an entire area that is prone to alien visitation, abduction, and electromagnetic shifts? The body of evidence is still out there somewhere in sands and rocks of the Oregon Coast.

PROJECT HOMUNCULUS: PREPARING FOR THE ALIEN WAR

"To it thou are Sole God and Lord, and it must serve thee." –
Alister Crowley

When I gaze out of that hypothetical window, out into the world around me, I am starting to feel a little disturbed. I am disturbed because what I am beginning to see is self fulfilling prophecy materializing on a daily basis. Prophecy that was talked about maybe 20 or 30 years ago showing signs of coming true.
The prophecy was not delivered by a prophet, or some dime store seer on a talk show, but it is prophecy that was first delivered by the millions of people who have either encountered or have seen something that they could not explain.

I have already determined that our government, and the media have taken advantage of the fact that our collective memories do not register the small details, of the stories that have been regarded as delusional, or Psychotic in the mainstream consciousness.

It is no surprise to the reader who is awakened that the "truth" gets redefined every day. But there are some who continually feel that these encounters and strange occurrences only happen to the easily duped, or the uneducated.

They conclude that the falsification of a story of little green men can not be readily figured out. They are only half- right.

It can be told and retold to sell books, movie rights, and ticket sales at modern day medicine shows where late night talk show hosts can

75

peddle their snake oils and verbal tonic water. Some stories eventually get dumped, and whether you know it or not UFO people police the fraternity, and sometimes they eat their own. The territorial backbiting and smear campaigns are numerous, like one religion bad mouthing the other.

People want you to believe that they have the ultimate truth, but a true researcher realizes that one way of thinking only remains fashionable for a short time, and then a new way of thinking takes it's place.

This is why it is important to tell someone who is even thinking about coming forward with a story about any kind of strange encounter that speaking of little green men doesn't always generate other green men on dollar bills.

Contrary to popular belief, people who see UFO's, who claim Alien abduction, or those who come out and admit to any kind of paranormal encounter are not at all wealthy and some have more problems that they have to deal with after they confess to their alleged encounters.

They are laughed at and ridiculed by colleagues and are always the butt of jokes in the mainstream media. It is always the consensus that the stereotypical alien "expieriencer" is a dullard who lives in the sticks somewhere.

The media likes to focus their cameras on these people because they know that it fortifies their position that there is no evidence to support UFO encounters.

The mainline media sources need to step up and acquaint themselves with the new attitudes that are being espoused by even the most ardent skeptics. A change is now occurring in the scientific community, as it begins to recognize that there is a complex and provocative body of, evidence, including physical evidence, connected with UFO sightings.

Reports are leaking out and are finding themselves in magazines that are not necessarily prone to reporting the "unknown" or "anomalous."

Magazines such as Popular Mechanics have taken the UFO question into practical evaluation by demonstrating that there have been secret Military operations where Saucers, and exotic aircraft have been used in Military exercises.

Ground Zero also attempted to bring the UFO story to a practical edge by coupling the military and exotic craft in the article "Secret Eye of the Triangle." It was eventually published in UFO Magazine.

This of course was followed up with an article investigating the Bentwaters case in England where soldiers were called out to investigate a strange UFO that had landed in the Rendelsham Forest during the Christmas Holiday week in 1980.

When I look at cases such as these I research the coincidences involved with each case. What they mean, and whether or not they are duplicated in any way.

However what I always run into are those who need an immediate narrative and they are expecting me to believe that all of my answers are solved in one concise article.

This is frustrating because the UFO and alien phenomena are still a puzzle. It can be all alien and paranormal, or unexplained experimentation, psychological manipulation, or a little of all of what I have mentioned.

There have been many people who have told us that the alien threat is a manufactured threat, something that can be used as leverage to create a fully cooperative world Government. Alien ideologies have been proposed for decades and an all out infiltration and infestation has been supposedly been ongoing since the 1940's.

It is alleged that the New World Order has been in process since the 1700's with the secret organizations such as the Illuminati and the Skull and Bones societies. There have been many people placed in positions of power to carry out these alien ideologies bent on control. The most notorious of course was the Third Reich and while we allegedly put that monster to bed, its tentacles seem to be very much alive and it's alien presence reveals itself in every way.

The "order" itself seems to be inspired by what seems to be an alien presence that has somehow creeped into the public consciousness. It seems to mirror what Jack Finney describes in "The Body Snatchers." The whole idea sounds very Science fiction and it can be rejected outright, or you can absorb it with critical thinking combined with an open mind.

The final stages of the total consolidation of the New World Order are about to take place. A lot of people claim that they would rebel at the proposal, but there are secret weapons and tricks that can be used to insure that people will goosestep to the company way if it means their death, or worse the harm of their families.

But how does a small group of individuals get a larger herd to follow without any question? Without any rebellion?

"Our differences world wide would vanish if we were to face an alien threat from outside this World"—President Ronald Reagan

An Alien threat? It's brilliant! Fearful humans would bow down to a living Extra Terrestrial Biological Entity coming down from the skies in a ball of fire!

Skeptics and some scientists still believe that this is improbable. They wonder how anyone with their wits about them could fall for such a crazy notion.

Well It's simple, with the gradual integration of the alien idea into the human psyche new behavioral and mental coping mechanisms emerge in the general populace.

Any schoolchild can draw you a picture of an alien - even though there is no convincing evidence that aliens have visited earth, or that they even exist at all. But an image of extraterrestrial beings exist, regardless of whatever reality you latch on to. They are as pertinent in a child's mind as Santa Claus.

In the adult psyche an alien image can share the same nebulous reaches of the mind with an unseen God. It's a convenient and sterile image as well. We all have an idea as to what God looks like. The renaissance painters have given us the graven images. However it would be logical to assume that God looks nothing like those images, and if a God would appear he would have to be in the image of man, animal, or of nature.

So we have already been conditioned to recognize an alien or a God if we happen to see one. Just who is responsible for the alien image is anyone's guess. The image could truly the work of someone with an over active imagination.

Then again the alien itself could be very real.

Let's go back to the mid 40's before the alleged Roswell event.

The story goes that L.Ron Hubbard, famous for his Science fiction stories like "Battlefield Earth "and founder of the Scientology program worked on a special project with Jet propulsion scientist John Whiteside Parsons. John Whiteside Parsons, usually known as Jack, first met Hubbard at a party in August 1945. After Hubbard left the Navy he ended up living in a trailer in Parson's back yard.

Parsons was not only a chemist who had helped set up Jet Propulsion Laboratories he was also s one of the innovators of solid fuel for rockets.

Parsons had an even darker secret. Parsons had an obsession with alleged Black magician Alister Crowley's Sex Magick.

He was the head of the Agape Lodge of the Church of Thelema in Los Angeles. The Agape Lodge was an aspect of the Ordo Templi Orientis, the small international group headed by Crowley.

After becoming Business partners and almost going broke Hubbard and Parsons agreed to do a Magik ritual. Parsons and Hubbard together performed their own version of the secret eighth degree ritual of the Ordo Templi Orientiis in January of 1946. The ritual is dealt with "the secret marriage of gods with men" or the "Babylon Working."

Hubbard and Parsons were attempting the most daring magical feat imaginable. They were trying to incarnate the Scarlet Woman described in the twelfth chapter of the Book of the Apocalypse in the Bible.

It was speculated that they wanted to create a Goddess that would sexually please them. They would have intercourse, impregnate the woman and then she would give birth to the moonchild or the servant boy child known as the "homunculus."

A similar ritual was in Crowley's book called the "Moonchild" where Crowley claims that a ritual can be performed to create the "Homunculus" in which the adept seeks to create a human embodiment of one of the energies of nature. It was Crowley's homunculus that resembled a little silvery man that he controlled and asked to his bidding. According to Thelemic legend, in 1918 Aleister Crowley came into contact with an interdimensional entity named Lam.

Lam was grayish in color and looked like a silvery gray child with deep dark eyes and cold skin.

It was Crowley who said in the Ritual "To it thou are Sole God and Lord, and it must serve thee."

It was the use of Black magik and the marriage of unknown forces to allegedly bring alien drones into the world. Men who in the image of nature would follow the adepts every command.

Hubbard and Parsons allegedly opened a gateway in their interdimensional rituals and the silvery beings created in the image of nature flooded our reality. There also seemed to be a change in attitudes and behaviors of the world after the doorway was allegedly opened.

Hubbard and Parsons eventually parted ways but their mystery lingered.

Hubbard of course started Scientology but Parsons history is shrouded in tales of alleged orgies, drugs, and child molestation.

Parsons was a great contributor to rocket science and his contributions to NASA and space exploration were vital. Parsons died in a lab accident in 1952. Parsons was memorialized with a statue at JPL and also had a crater named after him on the Dark side of the moon.

Now that both Hubbard and Parsons are dead it's time to ask, Did they succeed in opening a portal or door way? Did something get through the doorway?

It's coincidental that Kenneth Arnold saw his shiny discs one-year after the alleged ritual. It's highly spooky when you hear of little gray men piloting saucer shaped craft over the New Mexican desert and then having them crash land after the perverted Crowley Ritual allegedly took place.

If Black magic rituals weren't enough to shift the awareness to alien philosophies perhaps drugs and mind control could speed up the process.

We have already reported on projects that were once classified like ARTICHOKE, MK-SEARCH, and MK-ULTRA where mind control experiments were carried out on human test subjects by the CIA, NASA, The office of naval Intelligence, The Atomic Energy Commission and the Defense Advanced Research Projects Agency or DARPA.

Nazi's who were bored and needed to make mischief were conspiring with U.S. intelligence officers making the CIA even more powerful and creating the paranoia that resulted in the Cold War.

Nazis also come from a heritage rich in alleged alien, and supernatural magic. A daisy chain that when connected shows all kinds links to Men in Black, The Green dragon Society, The order of the Golden Dawn, and the Thule Society.

Hitler himself had allegedly been visited by a gray entity that only he could see. The entity would allegedly ask for more humans for experimentation. This would be connected to the alleged pact that exists between secret sects within governments like the CIA, who most fringe groups claim, permit that widespread human abductions continue, in return for secret alien technologies.

Is this a silly paranoid delusion?

Is all of this the result of such mental tampering? Perhaps psychological warfare? One can only speculate. However it seems that when we connect the dots we certainly see synchronicities that seem to unravel showing connection after connection or in the words of the late Jim Keith tentacles leading to one giant octopus.

I remember reading that after the Saucer fascination of the 1950's there were some groups who feared that a preoccupation with such things could lead to subversive behavior, behavior that could bring down religion and patriotism.

The Robertson Panel was formed by the CIA in the mid 1950's. They met in the Pentagon and devised a plan to dismiss any and all UFO reports. It recommended that since the information of UFO's and space visitors could cause groups to unite and create subversive behavior that it would be in the best interest to create Anti UFO education campaigns.

The way to implement such education was through the mass media. They even wondered if the Walt Disney company could produce anti UFO cartoons. Obviously the threat of alien ideologies was a real one.

The panel deemed the alien threat as a cancer to the orderly function of the body politic. Of course in the 1950's a U.S. news and world report article claimed that The US government had built a flying Saucer in 1942 and tried to explain that the various Martian sightings were the U.S. Saucers.

However there are claims that even though attempts were made to give sober reporting about Flying saucers, the military was secretly encouraging a belief in UFO's and Martians piloting these strange aircraft.

There are many UFOLOGISTS that will claim that this theory is completely wrong. They fully believe that the military is responsible for a cover up.

I often wonder if there is no real organized cover-up. I theorize that sometimes an outrageous claim is dismissed for it's complete lunacy. We all know as researchers in anomalies that any argument that is set out to prove a falsehood is immediately used as fodder to circumstantially prove that someone is trying to silence you, or cover up the "truth."

So of course circular logic tells you that just because someone tells you that perhaps you are off base—doesn't mean that they are organizing a cover up.

If there was a true cover-up then why is it that Aliens are in our pop culture? They are recognized Icons that are as identifiable as the Smiling face that said "Have a nice day" in the 1970's.

It must be made clear that the Hollywood Entertainment complex, (the group responsible for exposing us to different ways of thinking and fantasy) has churned out an infinite number of movies, books, and TV shows that have entertained the idea that aliens are indeed a reality, or at least a reality that needed to be accepted just in case they showed up on our doorstep.

Klatu baradda Necto , Live long and Prosper, Nanoo- Nanoo all alleged alien phrases and all part of our lexicon thanks to Hollywood. Bibles and Shakespearean plays are now being translated into Klingon, an alien language developed for a Television show and Movie.

Aliens with large eyes, big heads, and see through brains jumped out in 3-D in theatres and drive-ins all over the United States.

Saucers were seen in Hollywood movies, and the western world was putting a new face on the beings that came from the skies. In the movie Independence day a large UFO hovers over the Whitehouse and then with a green pulse of elctro-magnetic energy pulverizes the

White house sending the signal as to just who is in charge. It sent the message as to who would eventually rule. It even bothered Capital hill. Senators had mentioned that it was unnerving to sit and watch people cheer as the UFO destroyed an Icon of Democracy.

The message was sent loud and clear that they arrived and that they were very real. Later would hear that the alien reality was kept in the most hushed secrets by Military personelle.

There is even an Urban legend that claims that after Ronald Reagan watched a private screening of Spielberg's "ET The extra Terrestrial" he leaned over and whispered that "Many people are unaware just how close to the truth this is."

Reagan isn't the Only Leader who has hinted at possible Intelligent living outside this planet.

In the 1950's and 1960's people in key leadership positions began to blow the lid off the big secret.

Major Donald Keyhoe was speaking during a live broadcast on CBS when his audio was cut off:

"For the last 6 months we have been working with a congressional committee investigating official secrecy concerning proof that UFO's are real machines under intelligent Control."

Rear Admiral Roscoe Hillenkoetter who directed the CIA from 1947-1950 spoke openly about the UFO reality:

" Behind the scenes High ranking airforce officers are soberly concerned, but through official secrecy and ridicule, citizens are led to believe that UFO's are nonsense."

Other residual effects were stories told by prominent people of their encounters with aliens too.

One of the documented stories of famous people and their encounters with aliens and UFO's is the story of The Great One,

Jackie Gleason and his secret meeting with his golf buddy, president Richard M. Nixon.

President Nixon personally took Gleason to a secret location at an airforce base , and showed him the mangled remains of a flying saucer and dead aliens.

This story has not only been told by his x-wife Beverly but also Larry Warren Airman first class, who you may remember was involved with the Bentwaters UFO case.

It has all the classic connections with the Military and even a U.S. President.

According to a copyrighted story by Timothy Green Beckley, Warren and Jackie Gleason were having a few drinks when the story of the Bentwaters case came up. It was a casual conversation about UFO's and eventually evolved into the story that was first reported in the national Enquirer and later confirmed.

Gleason divulged his story about Aliens, Nixon, and the time when he was on a base viewing the bodies of the aliens.

"It was back when Nixon was in office that something truly amazing happened to me. We were close golfing buddies and had been out on the golf course all day when somewhere around the 15th hole, the subject of UFOs came up."

According to Gleason Nixon knew about them, and had an interest in aliens but didn't really go on about the details he truly knows.

Later that night Nixon shows up at Gleason's House alone without the secret service. He told Gleason to get into his car. They sped away and ended up at the gate of an airforce base.

"We drove to the very far end of the base in a segregated area finally stopping near a well-guarded building. The security police saw us coming and just sort of moved back as we passed them and entered the structure. There were a number of labs we passed through first before we entered a section where Nixon

pointed out what he said was the wreckage from a flying saucer, enclosed in several large cases.

Next, we went into an inner chamber and there were six or eight of what looked like glass-topped Coke freezers. Inside them were the mangled remains of what I took to be children. Then - upon closer examination - I saw that some of the other figures looked quite old. Most of them were terribly mangled as if they had been in an accident."

So if we are to believe Jackie Gleason's story President Nixon knew about the aliens or perhaps he wanted to convince Gleason of their existence by taking him to a military facility where they could be seen.

Why was he shown these beings? Why was Nixon the man to allegedly show him the UFO Imagery?

Is there some alien agenda that some powerful group secretly wants to encourage and other groups want to discourage? Why is it important to pick and choose a few people to carry that message? At what lengths will they go to promulgate an all out UFO Obsession? Is it a conditioning process for the reality? Or is it a conditioning process for a mass psychological experiment?

"The Main effect of UFO's on their witnesses is a conditioning process , through exposure to it's powerful imagery, man appears to be acquiring new forms of behavior and new models of his relationship to the world of nature."—Jacques Vallee

Jacques Vallee is a French astronomer who is well known amongst UFO enthusiasts and was actually the inspiration for the French astronomer Lacombe in Spielberg's Close Encounters of the third Kind.

"To conclude that UFO's are nothing more than secret devices deployed by some intelligence agency would be wrong and simplistic however there is some sort of genuine technology behind UFO's and if that technology is not the product of humans it is being manipulated by ingenious humans toward a cryptic end."—Jacques Vallee

This once again leaves us with the question are the UFO's man made? Are they extra terrestrial? Or are they extra terrestrial and man has found a way to use them to bring about a new space age religious order?

You can laugh at the prospect, but you can also see in history how claims of supernatural supremacy can lead to people following a centralized leader and obeying their laws becoming the very thing that Crowley spoke about when he talked of beings who follow your will.

Moses had his burning bush, his thundering mountain and his Ten Commandments. The children of Israel followed, some out of fear, others out of devotion to an unseen extra terrestrial god.

Mormons follow a centralized leader who testifies that Joseph Smith is a Prophet of God. Why? Because he was visited by beings from space that claimed to be God the father, Jesus Christ, and Moroni who was the angel who gave young Joseph the Gold plates with glyphs that eventually became the Book of Mormon.

Today over 9 million Mormons follow a prophet and are members of a church that is a model for a theocratic New World Order. The Mormon system provides many things for you, if you swear allegiance to its dogmas.

The LDS Church has welfare programs, money systems and laws that govern them. The church is worldwide. There are no borders that separate them (in spiritual terms) they are brothers and sisters in God.

Could UFO's and the alien threat be the conditioning mechanism to establish a New World Order capable of dissolving borders and uniting people into a totalitarian regime?

Can it be possible that if governments had the knowledge to create a "vision" of these extra terrestrials could it have successes similar to perhaps Scientology or Mormonism?

Perhaps.

If you look at groups such as Heaven's gate, The Branch Davidians, The Peoples Temple among others you see that there are some growing pains that come with brainwashing and mind control that goes awry.

Many always bring up the Heaven's Gate cult, because of all of its dogmatic worship of Gods who appeared to be alien. It also had computers and Science fiction, all glamorized during the 1990's in movies like "Independence day" and TV shows like the "X-files" and "Star Trek. The "crew" of the Higher Source cult was called an away team, similar to the crew of the Star ship Enterprise.

Remember there are popular Conspiracy theories that demonstrate that all of these bad religious/ alien tests were actually created by our own Government. Jim Jones, Marshal Applewhite, Charles Manson, all allegedly had ties to CIA mind control experimentation. Each leader was able to convince his followers that he was "divine" because of some direct connection to God, or aliens. Each group that followed them ended up dead, or in jail.

It's the cryptic end that Vallee speaks of.

The UFO phenomena could very well be the result of Illusion, and Magic created by those who know how to manipulate you. They know the secrets of the Alien threat. They can control it, because as Crowley says that the "homunculus " must serve its creator. Even so, there is no guarantee that a slave couldn't rise up against its master and revoke its pact.

If the aliens are unpredictable, and have their own agenda, then mankind can always use what they know about them to fool you into servitude. If a menace came down from heaven and terrorized the planet it would be easy to concoct some plan to neutralize them. If they have that knowledge then that would give them power.

Man has used the secret of God as a powerful control mechanism for millennia. Now there is a new creature in heaven and it can also be abused.

Norio Hayakawa is convinced that a secret diabolical cabal, will stage an extra terrestrial threat or event that will cause worldwide panic. This will then bring about the dissolving of borders and marshal law. Solidifying a totalitarian New World Order.

On what does he base his claims?

He bases his claims on something called the Phoenix Project that was outlined in a 1997 article that is posted on his website:

The March 31, 1997 DEFENSE WEEKLY ran a story, "Air Force Organizes For Offensive Info War". According to the article, the US Air Force has created the position of deputy director for information operations.

An "Offensive Information Warfare" division will be created under the new deputy director. The division will have the organizational code AF/XO1OW and will be headed by Lt. Col. Jimmy Miyamoto.

Offensive information warfare, which implies attacks on both military and civilian targets, is among the least discussed aspect of the Air Force's moves to organize, train and equip the service for information dominance, the article admits.

The new information Operations office will coordinate with the Pentagon's Joint Chiefs of Staff, National Security Agency, Defense Intelligence Agency, National Reconnaissance Office, Defense Airborne Reconnaissance Office and National Imagery and Mapping Agency.

New research efforts are under way to support this new program, including:......

Lethal HPM munitions. The USAF Office of Scientific Research is working on developing a small affordable laser and high-powered microwave for unmanned aerial vehicles (*UAVs - such as the ones possibly being tested at Groom Lake Complexes (AREA 51) in Nevada, General Aerodynamics facility by El Mirage Dry Lake, north of McDonnell-Douglas radar cross-section site near Llano, California,

Fort Benning, Georgia, covert facilities in Utah, etc. etc.) to perform a wide variety of missions, including enemy communications and computer systems.

Software viruses: to be placed or injected into enemy weapons and information links. These viruses would remain dormant until activated by satellite, aircraft radar, or jamming equipment, etc. When activated, the virus would render the equipment useless, or better yet, "there could be a very subtle change for a finite period of time".

Holographic projection: The article describes a quasi-information warfare/psychological operations program that was first discussed in the Air Force after Desert Storm. Holographic projection involves projection of a three-dimensional holographic image in project decoys, or even an "angry god" (religious imagery) above the battlefield. The Pentagon had listed the holographic projections openly as part of its "non-lethal" weapons program. But since 1994, the program has disappeared from view, evidently now a "BLACK" effort, says DEFENSE WEEK.

In conclusion, the DEFENSE WEEK article states that the Army's JFK Special Warfare Center and School in late 1991 disclosed that it was looking to develop a PSYOPS Hologram System with a capability to "project persuasive messages and three-dimensional pictures of cloud, smoke, rain droplets, buildings(*or, for that matter, even "flying saucers" and religious "figures").......The use of holograms as a persuasive message will have worldwide application". (This looks like it will be a concentrated unit of soldiers armed with the very latest high-tech weapons systems).

Coincidentally there are many believe that a test or simulation actually took place Over Phoenix Arizona on March 13th, 1997. There were many creepy coincidences that happened on that date. NORAD was on full alert for some reason on that night. Military exercises were happening on that night too. It was as if someone was expecting an arrival. A large UFO allegedly appeared in the sky over the city. Many claimed it was flares, others say it was a huge Mothership. A large flying triangle appearing over the city of Phoenix!

Its no wonder that ten days later, when Comet Hale-Bopp came closest to earth, The members of Heaven's Gate cult thought that a spaceship of extraterrestrials was behind the comet. Their beliefs prompted them to perform a mass suicide.

Some say that Project Phoenix was carried out by some clandestine operation. They point to numeric coincidences such as the date (March 13th) and the location (Phoenix). There are those who say that in secret societies the 'phoenix' symbolically represents a rebirth or resurrection. From destruction comes life.

These are frightening coincidences! I don't create 'em I just relate 'em

The idea of the military simulating a paranormal apparition to get a response is highly probable.

Silent weapons, which use electronic pulses can create all kinds of reactions from super heated skin, rage, paralysis, and hallucinations.

The Phoenix case appears to be a civilian test with Military cooperation.

However there are other cases where the Military could have conducted an alien simulation experiment on it's own soldiers.

A seldom-reported Incident at Fort Benning Georgia in 1977, could have either been a real alien attack, or an alien simulation attack. Probability points to the latter but Ground Zero has been speaking with a possible participant in the simulation.

Rob McConnell the paranormal investigator from Canada acquainted me with a former special forces paratrooper named Ted. For the sake of his anonymity Ted was called Ted IV.

In May of 1977, Ted had been in the Army for about four months, stationed at Fort Benning Georgia.

He was in paratrooper training with the 82nd Airborne, an elite Special Forces division made up of soldiers from all four branches of the service known as the Black Berets. His company was called to formation and volunteers were requested for an unexplained but highly classified mission. Ted and about 15 others were loaded into a cattle truck and taken to an old military facility.

The men did not know where they were. Ted assumed that they could have been in a place known as the "Troupe-Heard Corridor" a place that he says is a notorious area for UFO sightings and other strange events.

Ted claims that the men involved did not know each other. They wore no nameplates, and were not allowed to speak during the journey.

At the facility they were put through a battery of tests to evaluate their physical and psychological fitness. The strange part according to Ted is that they also tested acute psychic abilities.

The chosen few were taken to another room and briefed on what their mission was. He was told by an authoritative figure who claimed to be a sergeant (He wore black with no insignia) that President Carter, his family and friends were under threat of a terrorist attack in retaliation for his attempted rescue of the American hostages in Iran.

He was told that Ted's unit was going to be sent to guard the town of Plains because according to the sergeant "people were disappearing, animals were being mutilated, and strange lights were seen in the area.

The unit was on alert for foreign terrorists. However Ted claims that the story changed.

The strange lights and objects being reported in the sky were not from some foreign terrorist group. They were actually alien spacecraft. Ted was being told that he was being called to defend his unit against an alien invasion!

His orders were now from President Carter. The orders were shoot to kill.

Ted claims that he was with Bravo team and remembers 3 civilians running up to him and yelling "They are here, they are out to kill us all!" Ted was about to shoot at one of them but they were armed too.

They kept telling Ted to run.

Then as Ted was trying to radio his base, the radio wouldn't work. He looked ahead near and saw what looked like a strange glowing object.

Ted saw a greenish-yellow glow and stared in amazement. A creature was materializing in front of his eyes!

Ted told Ground Zero that the creature was hairless, and amorphous yet somehow had a humanoid form that undulated like a jellyfish. It had large, almond-shaped eyes, a lipless mouth, thin limbs with long fingers.

He doesn't remember seen in a UFO, but he remembers waking up in a hospital room with a priest giving him last rights. He was told that he served his country well, and that he would be given high honors. He has vague memories of being in a UFO crash. He was taken aboard a craft and that craft was shot down.

John T. Vasquez insists that an event similar to the one that Happened to Ted IV happened at Fort Benning in September of 1977. This experience would become the basis for the book "Incident at Fort Benning.".

He claims that on September 2nd, 1977 the 1st Battalion was assembled for a meeting with the company commanders and battalion commander. Vasquez says that four companies were present: Alpha, Bravo, Charlie and Delta. He was in Delta Company and has medical records to prove it.

During a parade at the camp, the battalion that Vasquez had just joined was also subjected to a UFO encounter that sent the parade ground into a state of anarchy. The men present were affected physiologically and psychologically, and Vasquez even reports telepathic contact by the intelligence behind the strange lights.

The bizarre exercise culminated in a battle with a UFO, and an encounter with an unknown entity. Vasquez relates that there were a number of tests that they were subjected to where they had to use super human ability, like psychic powers.

Like Ted IV, Vasquez is convinced that he came in contact with an alien presence.

Does this sound familiar?

It should, because one can remember the account of what happened at the Bentwaters facility in Suffolk, England. A listener of the Ground Zero Media show called the Program featuring Georgina Bruni who has been investigating the incident at Bentwaters and said that it most definitely happened.

The listener was ten years old at the time and he remembers that the base was on full alert for a "Broken Arrow" a term that means that a nuclear weapon is loose somewhere in the facility.

Was it a nuclear device? Or was that a cover term to keep people away from a base that was truly being invaded? Could it have been a smokescreen for a PSYOPS mind control test? Was it a test that included a possible simulated encounter with an extra terrestrial entity?

Other cases that have strange connections to these are the claims of Dan Sherman who appeared on Ground Zero to talk about Project Preserve Destiny. While working for the NSA Sherman was told that his Mother was visited in 1960, by an alien being.

Sherman was told that random tests were being conducted on the general populace at the time to determine compatibility." His superiors explained that while Sherman was in his mother's womb, he had received an implant that would give him the capability of communicating with aliens. He was to develop intuitive capabilities in order to carry out the task. However he never saw an alien, and he was told that his communications over the computer were done with alien intelligence.

Was this another PSYOPS program carried out by the NSA?

"Project Preserve Destiny began in 1960. This was/is a project

with the goal of genetically manipulating human offspring so they would have the ability to communicate with an alien species. It is a joint effort (alien/human) in cooperation with one another. I am unclear as to the real reasons for this cooperation. I was told it was to provide an ability to carry on high level communications during an impending electromagnetic communication outage on a worldwide basis subsequent to a major catastrophe in the future." – Dan Sherman

One more case that I can recall where soldiers were subjected to remote viewing drills, and were told the Extra terrestrials were landing or were about to land was the case of the "Gulf breeze 6."

A news story appeared in the Setinel on July 19, 1990 said that 6 soldiers who went AWOIL from their post in Germany ended up in Gulf breeze Florida. They were later transferred to Fort Benning Georgia.

The soldiers actually were preparing for the rapture. They had come to gulf breeze because they heard of multiple UFO sightings in the area. In a scenario eerily similar to the Heaven's Gate Cult. The soldiers believed that the end of the world was about to happen. They all had their bags packed, and duffel bags ready as if they were preparing for a trip.

The Northwest Florida News printed this headline:

6 AWOL SOLDIERS SAY THEY AIMED TO KILL ANTICHRIST

Gulf Breeze - Six soldiers, reported by an unofficial military newspaper to be on a mission to kill the Antichrist, were charged Thursday with desertion from their intelligence unit in West Germany, Pentagon spokesman said. A friend also told another newspaper that one of the soldiers arrested in this Florida Panhandle city, a hotbed for UFO sightings, was interested in unidentified flying objects and wanted to attend a UFO convention in nearby Pensacola.

The five men and a woman, all members of the 701st Military Intelligence Brigade at Augsburg, West Germany are being held

at Fort Benning, Ga. They were arrested Friday and Saturday after police stopped one of them for a traffic violation. They were charged with desertion RATHER THAN THE LESSER OFFENSE of being absent without leave because they held top-secret security clearances, said Pentagon spokesman Pete Williams. Padilla said it will be up to the soldier's commanding officer to decide whether to hold a court-martial or take lesser administrative action.

During the compilation of all of these stories it is evident that these cases have similar connections. All seem to be PSYOPS operations involving soldiers who are manipulated into believing that they are a part of an extra terrestrial operation or battle. These simulations have left the soldier and even the civilian convinced that they have been in the presence of an Extra terrestrial being.

Another coincidence is that in the case of the Gulf breeze 6, Vasquez and Ted IV all include briefing at Fort Benning Georgia which is one of the facilities spoken of by Norio Hayakawa as an "Offensive Information Warfare" center where Phoenix Lazer technologies are used in battlefield simulations.

The Fort Benning Facility also houses the School of the Americas. A place where special operatives are trained to be assassins. Many important names in military history both famous and infamous have trained at Fort Benning.

Including Timothy McVeigh.

Now, what are we creating at the bases that are allegedly there to protect us?

Perhaps the new Homunculus. Maybe even an army of them.

An army of about 280 million.

AURORA

When I first saw the previews to the movie Cowboys and Aliens some kid that was in the audience yelled out "that's lame." I was not only annoyed by this, but I also thought the idea would be really cool. There really hasn't been too much coverage about the possibility of UFO's, and aliens on the wild frontier, however I knew better. I have read so many stories about alien or celestial events recorded by cowboys but the one that is most impressive is the story of the airship crash in Aurora Texas in the 1800's.

It probably would have been terrifying for the people in that small town to see something flying in the air and crashing to the ground, especially when the Wright Brothers wouldn't get off the ground for at least another seven years.

We take UFO stories for granted now. We dismiss them as hoaxes, tricks of film, unconventional aircraft but back then there was nothing like that. There was no photo shop, no alien memes being pumped into the zeitgeist through science fiction and movies, no black ops experiments. It was just an airship, cigar shaped and coming down to the ground eventually crashing and killing its pilot.

On April 19th, 1897 the Dallas morning news reported that a large airship had hit a windmill on the property of a Judge J.S. Proctor and crashed. After the townsfolk investigated the scene, it was found that the pilot, a small disfigured man with a large head was killed in the crash. The little being was given a Christian burial. Before the being was buried it was determined by a Fort Worth army officer that the creature was "not of this world" and it was determined that the man was from Mars.

Wreckage from the crash site was dumped into a nearby well located under the damaged windmill, much of the debris was also buried with the alien in the grave. A man named Brawley Oates, purchased the property in 1945. Oates improved on the property and decided to clean out the debris from the wells so that it would be drinkable. In 1957 Oates had developed a debilitating disease from drinking the water. There were others who drank from the well that developed hideous growths on their joints. The disease disfigured the people.

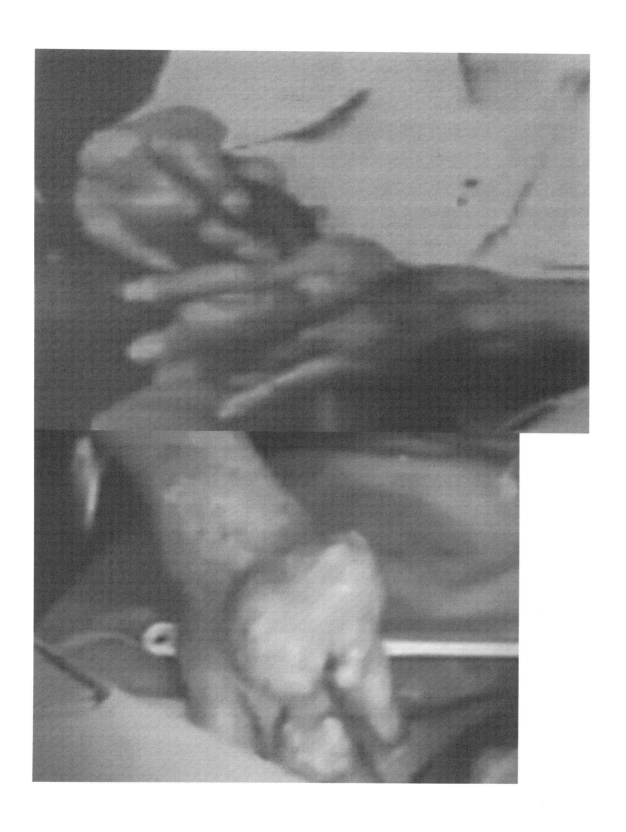

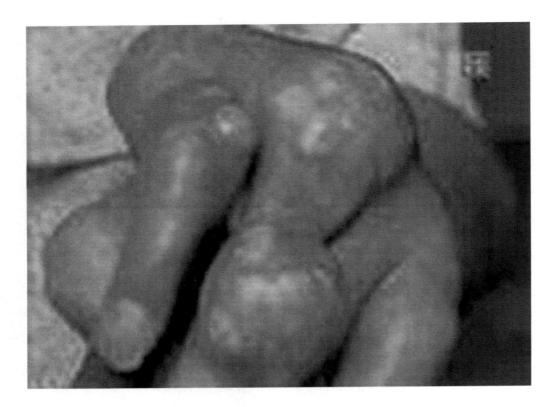

Oates decided to seal up the hole with concrete and built a small building on top of it. There have been many investigations into the incident and the Texas historical society has forbidden anyone to dig up the grave of the alleged spaceman. Jim Marrs who has written about the story extensively interviewed three living witnesses. One claimed the entire story was a fabrication to bring money to the town, while the other two witnesses said that the story is very real and that many people felt so sorry for the dead occupant in the ship.

Prior to this story – sightings of airships were reported in newspapers in San Francisco to New York that metallic cigar shaped airships were sighted in the sky. Airships were reported in Sacramento, Tacoma Washington, Hastings Nebraska, Chicago Illinois, Springfield Missouri, Decatur Michigan, and Waterloo Iowa.

Here we have a case of multiple sightings; over 108 were in Texas alone all at the end of the 19th, century. Texas UFO researcher Noe Torres and New Mexico historian John LeMay have recorded many encounters of aliens and airships in the old west. They claim that cowboys and farmers of the Old west had a hard time describing what they saw because spaceships and airplanes didn't exist. In 1864, a fur trapper named James Lumley claims to have seen an airship crash. He told a Cincinnati newspaper that the airship crashed. it was 'divided into compartments' and parts of it had been 'carved' with hieroglyphics, similar to the writings of ancient Egypt."

The sand surrounding the craft had been superheated to the point of creating what appeared to be glass.

Alien encounters have also been reported in the late 19th century. Although many of these encounters were described as angelic, there are at least two famous stories of being encounters that sparked major religious movements.

Mormon Church founder Joseph Smith, at age 14 claims to have been visited by beings on numerous occasions. Smith told stories of encounters with angels, even God and Jesus. His first vision was in a grove of trees where a bright line beamed down from the sky and told him to organize a new religion. Joseph Smith's encounters sound like typical alien abduction experiences you hear about today.

Smith was visited by an entity that said he was an angel. He told Smith to dig up Golden Plates and translate them from Egyptian Hieroglyphs. This translation eventually became the Book of Mormon the foundation for the Mormon Church's beliefs.

In the 1880's an American dentist, named John Ballou Newbrough claimed to have been visited by the Ambassadors of the angel hosts of heaven. The ambassadors told Newbrough to change his diet and write a book through automatic writing called the OASPE.

This book reveals that these Ambassadors come from the presence of the most high in heaven and come to earth in 3000 year cycles to teach mankind.

Later there would be another type of biblical work written by celestial beings called the URANTIA, however this book allegedly was revealed to a group of mediums in 1911.

If aliens were to arrive in the old west I am sure it would be the equivalent of God showing up and speaking. They had their bibles and their religion to try and interpret the experiences.

While UFO historians may have overlooked the old west as a time of UFO activity, there seems to be a lot of stories of angelic encounters and airship sightings that are anachronisms for the time.

Meantime we can sit in a movie theater and see what the mainstream may call an outrageous idea on the Hollywood screen.

MAJESTIC 12/12/12: THREAT OF THE MAGI

Sometimes during my broadcasts I have epiphanies that I really need to flesh out before I attempt to explain them to my audience. I was speaking with Rob Shelsky on 12/12/12 about a document that NASA has that seldom has seen the light of day and really doesn't get much fanfare. It is the R-277 document that serves as a chronological history of the moon.

If you read through the document you will find all kinds of interesting entries that make you really question just what goes on in outer space and whether or not there is indeed an intelligence apparatus that is constantly making the rounds and appearing in the skies.

I decided that maybe I should go back and reconsider some documents and programs that have always been part of UFO studies and have been controversial and event termed hoaxes by some researchers.

Some of the most controversial documents are the MJ-12 or Majestic 12 documents which allegedly shed some light on the real agenda of the extra terrestrial beings that were first recognized and brought forward in relatively contemporary history with result of the Roswell Crash in 1947.

Majestic 12 was a secret committee allegedly formed to develop government policy on alien life. There were many committees that followed afterwards, however Majestic had documented that the aliens were hostile and were most definitely a threat to the planet.

The Top Secret Operation Majestic-12 was established by order of President Harry S. Truman in 1947. Operation Majestic-12, was created to take charge of the technical, sociological and other aspects of the crashed UFOs and the small alien occupants, dead or alive, that were recovered. In later years this operation evolved into and became known as MAJI (the Majority Agency for Joint Intelligence).

MAGI is the most secret of all intelligence groups and out-ranks all other intelligence agencies including the National Security Agency (NSA) and the Central Intelligence Agency (CIA). MAJI is responsible directly and "only" to the President of the United States.

Within the report to Truman was an awful secret about the aliens they were using humans and animals for a source of glandular secretions, enzymes, hormonal secretions, blood and in horrible genetic experiments. There was also speculation that the aliens used human blood for nutritive value.

The other secret is that both Truman and late President Dwight D. Eisenhower had made deals or pacts with these beings that they could secretly experiment and abduct humans in exchange for highly advanced technologies that were later used in the Military industrial complex.

When a person reads over the accounts of some "intelligent or advanced" encounters throughout history, you begin to see patterns emerge. The patterns do not paint these intelligent or advanced beings in a good light. The reason is that these entities impart knowledge to mankind in most cases and for some reason that knowledge is used for a "militant" advantage.

It has been recorded throughout history that any paranormal reports of "contact" with gods or advanced beings have somehow coincided with the advent of war, genocide and conflict. Arguably, we can say that this has been the human condition for the last 6,000 years.

Rob Shelsky and another previous guest, Robert Steven Thomas, determined that perhaps war like aliens were responsible for the flooding of the earth and even the evidence that suggests atomic warfare existed anciently. It has been suggested that Vedic texts have indicated that ancient aliens may have fought wars using what we now call atomic weaponry to fight a destructive war.

I remember in 'Chariots of the Gods' that it was Erich von Däniken that believed that atom bombs destroyed Sodom and Gomorrah. There are many indications that this could be so, I would not be surprised if there would be a critical element that would try to debunk the idea. The remark is quite compelling.

In the book 'Gods from Outer Space', von Däniken mentions that old Indian and Tibetan texts in particular speak of lightning weapons, weapons of fire and weapons that use sound or frequency. There is also talk of bacteriological weapons being used as well.

Joseph Farrell has also written about the ancient pyramids being an ancient weapon of mass destruction. It's allegedly 'disarmed' at the moment, but it could possibly be used again as an ancient and effective tool of war.

Farrell theorized that the Great Pyramid was a terrible weapon of mass destruction, used by by a technological advanced ancient civilization in the mist of pre-history and sets today on the Giza Plateau disarmed but ready!

Farrell's technical civilization is the 'donor' civilization that provided the foundation of the Egyptian civilization that existed in the Nile Valley some 5,000 years ago.

What kind of civilization would have designed and built such an awesome weapon of mass destruction as envisioned by Farrell, and apparently used it with no hesitation against their fellow man?
A civilization not unlike those that arose from the foundations and ashes of older extinct civilizations. A civilization subject to all the faults and foibles of human beings, hatred, love jealously and greed. No different than those in existence today and poised to destroy the world.

Farrell speculates, the *"Great Pyramid was a phase conjugate mirror (magic mirror of legends),and howitzer, utilizing Bohm's 'pilot wave' as a carrier to accelerate electromagnetic and acoustical waves to a target via harmonic interferometer."* Ferrell believes that the chambers and passageways of the Great Pyramid were used as a series of loops to generate and amplify these gravito-acoustical waves and direct them to their target.

Farrell finds traces of this ancient science he calls "Paleophysics" in the ancient and obscure texts of Egypt.

If Ferrell's asumptions are correct, this ancient weapons system was the most powerful weapon ever to exist on Earth. Even today, with our advanced technology, the technology involved in the building of this weapon system can only exist in dreams. It also adds more fuel to the notion that the ancient aliens were involved with most of the calamities that have plagued over millennia.

I do know that William Bramley in his book The Gods of Eden had connected many dots and concluded that the basic causes of these wars, and the genocide is in part due to the less than benevolent interference of human affairs by extraterrestrials that make deadly and bonding deals with powerful individuals on earth. These beings regard human beings as property and end see earth primarily as an exploitable resource.

It takes an alien mind to continue the processes of war and to promulgate the process of torture and suffering. We have learned through the literature that has been created by whistleblowers that many of these advanced beings, that the "aliens" like the Annunaki were predatory and that they were known to drink the blood of humans.

Authors like David Icke had proposed that the Annuaki were blood drinkers and delighted in the suffering of human beings.

The Anunnaki drink blood, which they need in order to exist in this dimension and hold a human form . Embedded in this need lies another parallel between the Anunnaki and the figure of the vampire. The Anunnaki also feed off fear, aggression and other negative emotions.

Thus, while blood is needed as a vital life force, the Anunnaki are also addicted to "adrenalchrome," a hormone released in the human body during periods of extreme terror. Rather than sucking the blood directly from the necks of their victims, the Anunnaki apparently slash the throats of their victims from left to right and consume the blood out of goblets. "*In India,*" he writes, "*it was called soma and in Greece it was ambrosia, some researchers suggest. This was said to be the nectar of the gods and it was — the reptilian gods who are genetic blood drinkers.*"

This may or may not explain why there were those rumors in history about secret pacts with humans and aliens, more specifically the so-called collusion between the Nazi stronghold and the idea that the whole Reich was established under the direction of a malevolent alien force.

The German UFO era arguably can be traced to the Maria Orsic' contacts that began in 1917 and ended in 1945.

German scientists began working secretly on special Luftwaffe projects beginning in 1921- 1947 which consisted of various and numerous saucer projects, carried first by independent civilian German and Austrian scientists outside the control of the SS, and which later on became part of Nazi Germany wonder-weapons programs placed under the direct control of SS General Hans Kammler and SS General Jacob Sporrenberg, and few programs under the control of the Luftwaffe.

Maria Orsic's group tried to develop contemporarily saucer models and other super flying machines solely based upon channeled extraterrestrial technical data, while the other groups were attempting to build these experimental machines and develop new propulsion systems based exclusively upon scientific data, whether traditional or avant-garde using revolutionary concepts such as anti-gravity and harvesting energy from water, atom, oxygen, gas, liquid gas, various types of fuels, electro-magnetic field, and other unconventional sources and materials.

Thus, we have here an era which consisted of more than one German effort, one German group, or a specific direction toward developing and building UFOs. Each project and effort was carried out according to new concepts, theories and discoveries, quite often in sharp contrast with what was going on in various and separate facilities, hangars, military bases, underground testing tunnels, locations and laboratories.

The Vril, Thules and other groups allegedly found that they could generate from inanimate material "true" Aryan beings and these beings were able to teach Nazi engineers how to make a saucer shaped inter–dimensional time travel machine.

By 1932 Hitler had gained enough control of German society to force scientists to work in laboratories on saucer aircraft designs. Aided by the implosion vortex technology of Victor Schauberger, and the technical expertise of scientists like Schriever, Habermohl, Ballenzo and Miethe, the Germans were making extraordinary progress. The Germans, allegedly under the direction of the secret chiefs, were creating the first flying saucers.

Later the MJ-12 Documents were crucial in connecting the dots between the notorious torture of the Nazis and the later abduction and torture scenarios of the 1960's through the 1980's.

All these so called leaked" documents illustrate a recurrent theme that the Nazis had contact with alien technology that was used and exploited by the Soviet Union and the United States. The retrieval of crashed saucers and their occupants began in the late 1940s and a secret treaty with the aliens was made in the 1950s. Since then the aliens have broken this treaty and continued abducting people for the purposes of research and nutrition.

Most of the information about UFOS and aliens cannot and most assuredly is not what the New Age alien cultists are expecting because many have put faith in their discoveries and made them spiritual and faith-based, sometimes bordering on, or fully, a delusional response to the phenomenon. The alien phenomenon and the UFO exploration sometimes develops into some warped apotheosis that needs to be kept in check. Why is it that the majority is so quick to accept the phenomenon as a messianic delivery system from the woes of our existence when it becomes evident that the phenomenon is responsible for the same woes that we experience?

Believing there's something else "out there" (where ever that may be) that is largely unknown is one thing, but faith in specific attributes about that unknown thing, and avoiding the connection these being have to the cataclysmic model, is quite another.

Regardless of what we see, whether it is a fake rubber alien dummy being cut up on a television special or watching a facehugger grip its next victim we are now being educated in the revelation of the method. The alien worlds are hostile and the creatures are much like a vampires – or perhaps they are amoral and rely heavily on self preservation and therefore need human bodies for digestives. This type of thinking is not new, it is the age old opinion of the critical Fortean mind that does not trust the weirdness of this world that is destined for utter damnation on the road to Armageddon and the alien harvest.

NEW CLEAR ALIEN MESSAGE

It was reported on ABC news that there were at least 19 sightings of UFO's over the Great Lakes last night May 12th, 2011. The lights were in formation over Lake Michigan and families were calling the authorities to report there was what appeared to be a mini invasion over the lakes. It appears that UFO sightings are increasing in 2011 and with the aid of cell phones and video we are beginning to see that perhaps there are more lights and anomalies in the sky, So many in fact that the United Nations has developed protocols for announcing and even meeting with the extra terrestrials. All of this sounds a bit crazy, but the reality is that the world is preparing for the very real possibility of alien contact or intrusion.

It is important that you understand that there have been some anomalous developments taking place in space, developments that the western media has not reported thoroughly. In fact they have ignored these major developments for fear that it might panic that populace. It is important that we report these stories to you in order to demonstrate that we are most certainly preparing for the alien intrusion and that there are military personnel and others that are no longer keeping quiet.

Some of the secrets that are about to be revealed are mundane and others will confirm what we have speculated about for nearly 6 decades. The alien extra-terrestrial threat, from UFO's to NEO's are being taken seriously by our government.

Some people are turning to religion and believe that their beliefs are being threatened by the so called aliens. They are worried that they will be a replacement for their gods and denounce them as demons. It is important to illustrate that both Christian and Muslim faith have within the passages of their own scriptures, stories of aliens and special anomalies that have been recorded and being realized by a creator how has created all things.

With a rich history of denying science's explanations of the cosmos, the Catholic Church seems to be very fascinated with what is going on in space. Now stating that not only have they accepted the idea of alien life in space, they are now going to seek it out. Father Jose Funes, a Jesuit astronomer at the Vatican Observatory and said: "As a multiplicity of creatures exists on Earth, so there could be other beings, also intelligent, created by God. This does not conflict with our faith, because we cannot put limits on the creative freedom of God."

In the Quran it states; and indeed, We have created stellar formations in the form of spheres in the heaven and have beautified them for the onlookers, and have protected them from every outcast Djinn. Except him the devil that gains hearing by stealing, he is pursued by a clear shihâb.

It is believed that before the arrival of the Prophet Mohammad there were Djinn that would come down from the heaven's to eavesdrop on the prayers given at the stations of the ascent into the heavens. They would then pass these prayers on to sorcerers. There would be spheres that would fall from the heavens to stop the Djinn from doing their evil deeds.

It has been theorized that the word shihâb refers to either cosmic rays or dark matter. In Arabic we learn that the Djinn or demons are capable of shutting down stations between earth and heaven making them go silent. Could the Djinn be aliens that are capable of shutting down communications satellites or other machines in order to thwart the plan of mankind?

There was such an incident that has been recorded by Jim Klotz and Robert Salas where Missile silos protecting our country were shut down reportedly by UFO's that hovered near the site.

In central Montana, on March 16 1967, the E-Flight Missile Combat Crew was below ground in the Echo-Flight Launch Control Center (LCC) or capsule. During the early morning hours, more than one report came in from security patrols and maintenance crews that they had seen UFOs.

A UFO was reported directly above one of the Echo-Flight Launch Facilities (LF) or silos. It turned out that at least one security policeman was so frightened by this encounter that he never again returned to security duty.

A short time later, the Deputy Crew Commander, a 1st Lieutenant, was briefing the Crew Commander, a Captain, on the flight status when the alarm horn sounded. Over the next half-minute, all ten of their missiles reported a "No-Go" condition. One by one across the board, each missile had became inoperable,

An in-depth investigation of the E-Flight incident was undertaken. Full scale on-site and laboratory tests at Boeing's Seattle plant were conducted. Both declassified Strategic Missile Wing documents and interviews with Boeing engineers who conducted tests following the E-Flight Incident investigation confirm that no cause for the missile shutdowns was ever found.

The most that could be done was to reproduce the effects by directly introducing a 10 volt pulse onto a data line. One conclusion was that the only way this could be done from outside the shielded system was through an electromagnetic pulse from an unknown source.

In this case we have the shutdown of strategic nuclear missiles and a confirmed UFO sighting over a missile silo. These were missiles lost to America's nuclear deterrent forces.

USAF has confirmed that all of Echo flights' missiles shutdown within seconds of each other and that no cause for this could be found. For many years, the Air Force has maintained that no reported UFO incident has ever affected national security. It is established fact that a large number of Air Force personnel reported sighting UFOs at the time many of our strategic missiles became unlaunchable.

The incidents described above clearly had national security implications. In one previously classified message, SAC Headquarters described the E-Flight incident as: loss of strategic alert of all ten missiles within ten seconds of each other for no apparent reason and a cause for grave concern

This may indicate that the aliens have hostile intent and are quite capable of disarming us. There are those that will argue that they did nothing after they shutdown the missile systems – however the point is in the potentiality of harm and the risk to national security.

Flights of fancy about friendly angelic aliens and speculation make for some great stories, but reality is a bit more frightening. The extra-terrestrial threat or "disclosure" that everyone is waiting to hear about is going to inform us that we are about to come in contact with invaders and celestial bodies that will shake the earth to its core. They have the capability to shut down our vital systems of protection, and could open us up for an attack or even a collision with a natural body from space. Each year, over 300 objects intersect Earth's orbital trajectory. They range in size from a soccer ball, to the size of Manhattan. It is only a matter of time, before we arrive at the wrong place at the wrong time. We are also tracking a wave of extra-terrestrial anomalies from alleged wormholes, vortices, lights and spaceships that no one has seen before.

The sun is also very active and solar flares and CME's have also been determined to be grave threats to our way of life.

The US Office of Science and Technology Policy, which advises the White House, developed an emergency policy to address the asteroid hazard in October 2010 It is likely to be influenced by a report from the National Research Council about extraterrestrial threats. The report concludes that there is a potential for an extra-terrestrial event and that we need to create a budget for warning and tracking systems.

When Ronald Regan made his speech about the world uniting against the alien threat there were many people who claimed that he was senile and that he was only speculating about such matters.

The alien threat discussion was also brought up in a secret meeting with Soviet Leader Gorbachev.

Gorbachev himself confirmed the conversation in Geneva during an important speech on February 17, 1987,in the Grand Kremlin Palace in Moscow, to the Central Committee of the USSR's Communist Party. In the speech he stated that "Reagan said that if the earth faced an invasion by extra terrestrials, the United States and the Soviet Union would join forces to repel such an invasion. He then stated that he would not dispute the hypothesis, but included that he thought that it was too early to worry about such an intrusion. That was 23 years ago and perhaps at the time it was premature but now it seems to be a very real scenario.

It is interesting to point out that Gorbachev never spoke of how weird the conversation was, he only commented that it may be too early to talk about such an event as an alien invasion. Did this indicate that perhaps there is a date when it would be more appropriate to discuss these things? Or have the Governments of the world been planning on a date where they announce to the world that Life is out there in space? Is there a predetermined time where the United States government will remove all doubt about where we are in the universe?

When the time comes will you be psychologically prepared for it?

RETURN TO MAURY ISLAND

Some of the best UFO stories in my opinion are the ones with the backdrop of the Cold War. When flying saucers and flying discs were not meant to be called 'UFO's' and aliens were merely saucer men or little green men from Mars.

I guess there is always a soft spot in one's heart for the comic book versions of the flying saucer and the men from space. My father turned me on to some classic comic books that went beyond the stories of Batman and Superman. There were also other magazines that were pulp zines that talked about aliens and flying saucers all the time. In the 1950's and 1960's the flying saucer stories were fun and later into the 1970's and 80's what was simply a b-movie mythos became a topic of cover-up, conspiracy and film noir intrigue as the aliens were more than just imaginary villains, they were now a product of classified top secret intelligence.

The pulp and comic book fantasy became reality and the mystique became more and more horrifying as we began to hear in the nightly news reports stories of abductions and cattle mutilations.

I remember when I was growing up there were two terrifying stories that always had my attention. The first one was John Keel's 'Mothman Prophecies' where a giant human like flying creature terrorized a small town in the Ohio valley and The Maury Island Incident where two men and a young boy witnessed flying saucers near Washington state in 1947. The story was unbelievable and as a young man I really did not look into the details of the incident. As I grew older I wanted to know more about the case.

It wasn't until 1996 when I received a copy of the 'Big Book' of strange stories that I was once again reading a graphic novel telling the tale of what happened on the little peninsular island just outside of Vaschon Island, Washington in the American Northwest.

Many people are unaware that the very first reports of unidentified flying objects were in the Pacific Northwest.

Before stories of an alien crash landing in Roswell, New Mexico, before a pilot spotted UFO's near Mt. Rainier and before the UFO photos were taken near McMinnville, Oregon – there was the Maury Island incident in Puget Sound, Washington.

This was the beginning of the modern UFO era. Those early sightings were centered in Washington state and in Oregon.

When I lived in Utah, I was close enough to Area 51 and the west deserts of Nevada to visit areas where alleged UFO activity was happening. I was also close enough to Roswell and in 1997 I arrived there to celebrate the 50th anniversary of the Roswell crash.

Little did I know that I would find myself in a situation where I would move closer to the area where the Maury Island incident took place and the famous Trent Farm Saucer was taken.

I also happened to wind up in Bigfoot territory when I moved to the Pacific Northwest and found out that an old colleague of mine in Utah was being sought by the FBI because of the possibility of him being the infamous D.B. Cooper, a folk hero in the Northwest and a historical figure that remains a man of mystery.

When I moved to Portland, Oregon I wanted to first organize a trip to Maury Island. It would take me eight years to organize a group to investigate and by the time I was ready to go to Maury Island I collapsed and was rushed to the hospital and was later diagnosed with cancer. I waited another 5 years to organize another trip and in June of 2013 I was diagnosed again with cancer.

A year later, I decided that I was going to investigate the Maury Island case regardless of my health condition. The trip and the investigation was a success and even though I sprained my ankle during the investigation and the Vaschon paramedics had to rush me to South Harbor Hospital in Seattle I can say that I got what I was looking for and at the 15th, annual McMinnville UFO festival I am here to give my report to a national audience that I hope has the same interest as I do in the case.

On June 21st, 1947, harbor patrolman Harold Dahl was cruising in a boat near Maury Island in Puget Sound, Washington. Dahl had his 15 year old son and his dog along as they salvaged logs on that warm summer day.

Off in the distance, they spotted what they said were six round objects that resembled flying doughnuts. One of the objects was flying erratically and started descending towards the boat. Dahl said it began spinning and emitting bits of something that looked like lava or white hot metal. The slag hit the boat, breaking a worker's arm and killing the dog.

Dahl used the ship-to-shore radio, but there was too much interference to send an SOS. The panicked harbor patrolman had the presence of mind to snap a few photos as he steered towards shore on Maury Island. He took his son to a Tacoma hospital, to have the boy's burns treated. He later told his employer Fred Crisman, that he thought the metal ejecta had showered down from an alien space craft.

Later, Dahl claimed that he had been visited by what he described as a stereotypical man in black – or MIB. The man wore a black suit and drove a brand new Black Buick sedan. The MIB treated Dahl to breakfast at a waterfront cafe in Tacoma. While Dahl sipped his coffee, the mysterious visitor revealed that he also had witnessed the six UFOs. He told Dahl that if he loved his family he would keep his mouth shut about the whole affair.

The one person Dahl confided in was Fred Crisman, who was eager to see photographic evidence from the pictures Dahl said he had taken. It turned out, though, that the camera film was useless because the negatives were fogged. Crisman decided to check it out in person. He went to Maury Island and claimed to have seen metal slag strewn all over the ground. While he was surveying the area, a similar doughnut shaped object appeared out of the clouds. It was there, he said, right in front of him. In that moment, Fred Crisman became a firm believer in Dahl's story.

Later that summer, a team from the U.S. Air Force sent two investigators who visited Maury Island and collected samples of debris. They carried the material with them for a return flight to San Francisco in a B-25 aircraft, but never made it. On August first, 1947, the plane crashed near Kelso, Washington, killing the crew onboard.

It's a story partly gleaned from declassified FBI documents – a conspiracy investigation that the government wanted to hush up. Then came the mysterious military plane crash. What material was on board that B-25?

Whatever it was, it apparently was linked to what Harold Dahl claimed to have seen in the sky over Maury Island, as the first wave of UFO sightings began in the Pacific Northwest.

I remember that when I was in Roswell, New Mexico in 1997 I was making some connections to what happened with Dahl and Crisman and what Kenneth Arnold reported in 1947 while flying over Mt. Rainer. I also spoke with Stanton Friedman in Roswell about Maury Island and he discouraged me from investigating the case because he said it was a hoax.

In 2007, it was reported that a prospector hiking in the area of Rose Valley near the ravine in a forested area of Kelso found wreckage of the missing B-25. It was the first time I saw mainstream news reports speaking about a secret military plane crashes and most importantly an aircraft that carried a classified cargo—namely parts of a flying disc. Before I planned my first outing in Washington, I wanted to verify that what I was hearing was true. After I placed a call into the local news agency I was told that the wreckage in question was tied to a strange UFO story form 1947.

I thought, if this is a hoax then why is this place and wreckage find so important?

It was then that I realized that the story may have been called a hoax and that maybe Crisman and Dahl were forced to recant their story. I then wondered why so many people are hoping that the Maury Island story would go away when the proof of it all can be found in wooded area outside of Kelso, Washington.

I did some dot connecting and perhaps what we are dealing with is a story that if it was given any credence would be devastating for our military and our government, especially if the military pilots died carrying something that could be far more dangerous to national security if revealed.

As Weird U.S. writes in 'The Maury Island Incident':

"Dahl and Crisman sent a package to publisher Ray Palmer in Chicago. (A year or two later, Palmer founded Fate magazine.) The package contained a box of metal fragments and statements about the strange happenings on the 21st and 22nd of July. A few weeks later, Palmer contacted Kenneth Arnold (see Flying Saucers at Mount Rainier), who had begun investigating UFOs.

Arnold arrived in Tacoma in late July with airline pilot E.J. Smith. The two of them met with Dahl and Crisman, examined Dahl's boat, and conducted interviews. Dahl and Crisman did not produce the pictures, however. Dahl also told Arnold that his son had disappeared. (Dahl said later that his son was found waiting tables in Montana, but he could not remember how he got there.) On the afternoon of July 31, Captain Lee Davidson and First Lieutenant Frank Brown of the U.S. Army Air Force flew up to Tacoma from Hamilton Field, California.

In addition to being pilots, the two men were intelligence specialists. They met with Arnold, Smith, and Crisman for several hours. One of the officers said that he thought there might have been "something" to the story, but they had to leave around midnight. They were in a hurry to be at Hamilton Field on August 1, the day when the Air Force was to split from the Army. The two officers flew out of McChord Air Field around two o'clock in the morning on a B-25 bomber, with a crew of two other men. About twenty minutes later, the airplane crashed near Centralia, Washington. The two enlisted men managed to parachute to safety, but Davidson and Brown were killed, making them the Air Force's first casualties.

Dahl and Crisman said that the AF officers took some of the strange metal onboard. People thought they heard anti-aircraft guns shoot the plane down. The local newspapers and FBI received phone calls stating that the plane was shot down to cover up the information Brown and Davidson had found. Because of the loss of life, the Air Force broadened its investigation and the FBI launched their own.

The Air Force investigators determined that the crash had been a terrible accident. One of the engines caught fire and the men to began bailing out. Before Brown and Davidson could jump out, a wing broke and struck the tail section, which also broke off. The plane went into a spin, trapping the men inside.

Another Air Force investigator spoke with Dahl and Crisman and visited their boat. He stated that the damage he saw did not match the damage the two sailors described. There were no piles of metal on Maury Island, and the existing samples looked like slag from a metal smelter. His *conclusion matched that of the FBI investigator: that Dahl and Crisman had faked the incident to gain publicity for a magazine article.*

The FBI warned Dahl and Crisman that their hoax had not succeeded and that if they dropped the matter, the government would not prosecute the two men for the fraud, which had resulted in the deaths of the two officers."

You would think that a hoax which resulted in the deaths of two officers would be a prosecutable crime. Both men, however, were never charged in the deaths which puts into question the validity of the hoax story. It is also interesting to note that Fred Lee Crisman, one of the so-called hoaxers in the Maury Island case, had connections to a well-known and notorious name in our history, that name is Clay Shaw.

Clay Shaw was arrested and tried for complicity in the murder of John F. Kennedy, acquitted on March 1, 1969 by a grand jury.

If we dig into some interesting history we find that Clay Shaw was a spy for the OSS, the United States spy agency that preceeded the CIA. Shaw's spy business was also accompanied with his ties to Nazi POW's and 'Operation Paperclip' where the United States brought over from Germany Nazi scientists that were helping the war effort by providing information about rocketry and in some conspiracy circles secret saucer technology that was allegedly being tested by the Nazis.

Werner Von Braun first met Clay Shaw in 1945 when he, Walter Dornberger – soon to become the chairman of Bell Helicopter, and about 150 other Nazi rocket scientists abandoned Peenemünde and traveled south to join the American forces in Germany close to the French border.

As Alex Constantine wrote in 'Project Paperclip and the Kennedy Assassination':

"Von Braun first met Clay Shaw in 1945 when he, Walter Dornberger [soon to become the chairman of Bell Helicopter] and about 150 other Nazi rocket scientists abandoned Peeemunde and traveled south to join the American forces in Germany close to the French border. The Nazis

were brought to the Deputy Chief of Staff's headquarters where major Clay Shaw maintained their relationship over the years through their mutual connection with the Defense Industrial Security Command, or D.I.S.C., an operational arm of the counterespionage division of the FBI... When Shaw learned he was a suspect in the Garrison investigation, he immediately phoned one Fred Lee Crisman, a veteran of Operation Paperclip and a covert contract "security" specialist for aerospace firms."

Did Crisman hold a secret about classified Nazi saucer technology and was he trying to get the word out about our alliance with Nazi scientists and their so called alien technology?

If it was reported that the pilots that died in B-25 were carrying Nazi tech, wouldn't that have been a scandal so great that it would shake the nation two years after World War II?

At first, Dahl and Crisman went along with the whole hoax claim. They made statements that the story was a fake and simply refused to give interviews on the matter. But a few years later in the January 1950 issue of Fate magazine, Crisman stated that the incident had happened, and Kenneth Arnold included Maury Island in his 1952 book 'The Coming of the Saucers'.

As MUFON notes:

"Today, most people believe that Crisman and Dahl faked the incident, perpetuating a hoax that got out of control. Other people believe that the U.S. Government was behind a conspiracy that may have involved anything from UFOs to dumping nuclear waste in Puget Sound."

Perhaps the key to the whole UFO mystery goes far beyond that of Roswell and begins with shady relationships with Nazis, the aerospace industry and the very real possibility that stealth Nazi aircraft that was financed by prominent American investors was being seen in the skies during and after World War II.

The mystery of Maury Island remains just that, a mystery. And as outrageous as it may sound, we can't erase it from UFO history just because the story has a lot of inconvenient inconsistencies.

BLUE BOOK: THE 22 YEAR REGRETTABLE HISTORY

For 22 years, the military seemed to spare little expense in chronicling humans' reported otherworldly encounters with glowing orbs, spinning spheres, and flying triangles.

All of it had been hidden away in archive files until the government dumped 130,000 documents worth of BLUE BOOK material in a free online database for the first time last month.

The project launched in 1947, two years after the end of World War II and just as the Cold War was gearing up. It concluded in 1969 without offering definitive proof of either aliens visiting the Earth or advanced spy craft launched by our enemies. But the goldmine of reports —

witness names redacted — provides a snapshot of a nervous, suspicious era that drove our government to consider even the most outrageous reports.

Now with the articles and the top secret files no longer top secret we are now beginning to see a resurgence in interests about UFO's and we are also beginning to see ultimatums by governments and indications that top ranking US officials are more than ready to make the announcement that we are not alone and that we have been seeking information from these alien beings and it is with that information we have advanced in many technical leaps.

The public's imagination went wild with UFOs, in the forties and fifties and even though we are in the present are looking for disclosure, President Truman had already acknowledged the presence of UFO's. He never really went on the record to disclose who was piloting them, but he most certainly knew of their existence and the hysteria that they were causing around the country.

Between 1947 and 1957 radio and television broadcasts were interrupted by various saucer reports provided by Blue Book. It simply was the government doing a good job with public relations assuring the public that while there were many of these craft that could be explained there were still several that were very mysterious and most certainly had contact with the air force pilots that flew over the United States. It was a serious attempt to find if there was any validity to a UFO crisis or just mass hysteria.

For the Air Force, it was driven more over concerns that the Soviets created a super secret weapon than if there were little green men. However that did not stop reports of flying craft landing in various areas with occupants walking out of their various flying craft to see the earth. In the end, many of the more than 12,000 sightings diligently investigated by the Air Force were chalked up to weather phenomena, meteors, satellites, a bright planet, balloons, birds or overactive imaginations.

The latter category would seem to fit the story told in 1964 by the lost hunter near Lake Tahoe, who swore he spent the night in a tree, firing arrows at three white "robot"-looking creatures, setting scraps of his clothing afire and hurling the pieces at the glowing aliens below. Although the BLUE BOOK documents suggest the military's time commitment was considerable, it wasn't enough to please everyone. In 1966, then-Michigan congressman and future president Gerald Ford complained that the Air Force was dismissing scores of UFO sightings from his constituents as "swamp gas" and called for a Congressional inquiry into the phenomena.

He wasn't the only famous politician to get an earful from his constituents about UFOs. In a letter to President John F. Kennedy, 63-year-old Alice Reynolds of San Mateo, Calif., said she was out feeding bread to the birds when she saw two stationary white balls, one with a tail, in the early morning sky Nov. 13, 1961.

She complained that she tried to contact the Civil Defense Control Center in Belmont, but it wasn't open, so she called the police: "They were more curious as to why I (was) up at that time than what I called about," she wrote to the president.

The UFO witnesses ranged from grandmothers to amateur astronomers and even military pilots, who should have known a weather balloon when they saw one.

Several reports included sketches, charts and purported photographs of the objects.

By 1969 the UFO reports had dwindled and while reports were still coming in, reports now included stories of being abducted and harmed by the occupants of these flying craft.

There were also saucer parties that were organized where average everyday people would gather in remote areas to try and catch a rogue UFO on film. The footage would show lights in the night sky executing some extraordinary maneuvers.

In Dec. 17, 1969, the Air Force terminated the project, citing conclusions from a University of Colorado report titled, "Scientific Study of Unidentified Flying Objects." Researchers determined there was no threat to national security, additional scientific knowledge or extraterrestrial vehicles uncovered by Project BLUE BOOK. However, 701 sightings remain "unidentified."

After that it seemed that the military no longer wanted anything to do with UFO sightings and yet the sightings continued and stories of abduction were now being told with the first being told by Betty and Barney Hill.

In 1961 Betty and Barney Hill reported seeing a UFO and experienced a period of missing time while on a long car journey. Under hypnosis they both separately described how they were abducted by aliens and shown around the spacecraft before undergoing medical examinations. Betty also spoke of the origin of the aliens which were of the Zeta Reticuli system but at that time it wasn't discovered until 1969.

Of course this spun several similar tales of marauding aliens entering into homes and terrorizing people.

This raised questions as to what the aliens wanted. Were they truly here to help humanity or were they truly a threat.

According to some surveys nearly 2% of Americans believe that some strange intruder has abducted them. The abduction scenarios read like a recipe in most cases and there is also the same amount of people within the set of reported cases that are determined to be psychotic or delusional. The fact is that not every case is a true abduction case. This does not mean however that the phenomenon is not happening.
The handful of accounts that have no explanation are horrifying and deserve investigation.

If this kind of kidnapping and torture was carried out by a human agency there would be a consensus demand for an investigation into who or what was responsible.

Since such a small amount of people claim that these events are happening, governments have not investigated them.

There has also been the theory that world governments are involved with the abduction processes and that perhaps a collusion with aliens exists or the most horrifying of all, humans are carrying out these experiments and using the alien stories as a cover. After all, an "alien" would not be able to stand trial for these crimes against humanity. Abductees were claiming for many years that invasive procedures were being used for some higher purpose and that DNA was being sequenced in order to study humans. The invasive procedures included the removal of sperm, Ova, DNA, and human fetuses.

Abductees for many years were saying that they have seen firsthand that these aliens were able to extract sperm and ova from them but many claimed that they saw clones of themselves and clones of several other mammals in labs that were on ships. Many abductees made claims that the aliens were using their DNA to replicate alien hybrids. These cases were best known and heard in the early seventies and eighties. In 1984 President Ronald Reagan, who was also a Commander in chief with an obsession with apocalyptic matters admitted during a Presidential debate against Walter Mondale to having "philosophical discussions" about Armageddon in the White House with some well known evangelical ministers.

Reagan seemed to be speaking ex cathedra on four different occasions about extraterrestrial threats before the end of his presidency. Reagan even spoke with General Secretary Gorbachev in Geneva about world wide differences dissolving if we had to face of a universal extraterrestrial threat. Reagan's statements were confusing when on one hand he declared that the alien threat was already among us and that their agenda is war:

I occasionally think how quickly our differences worldwide would vanish if we were facing an alien threat from outside this world. And yet, I ask is not an alien force ALREADY among us? What could be more alien to the universal aspirations of our peoples than war and the threat of war?

While many of Reagan's comments were interpreted as ramblings about an alien attack, it can also be theorized that Reagan had his mind couched in apocalyptic thought and the possible threat of an asteroid or comet hitting the earth and causing a worldwide catastrophe. A threat from space would definitely humble the planet. It would be hoped that it would humble our leaders into becoming more aware of just how fragile our existence on this planet truly is. At the forty-second session of the UN General Assembly on September 21, 1987, President Ronald Reagan said:

"In our obsession with antagonisms of the moment, we often forget how much unites all the members of humanity. Perhaps we need some outside, universal threat to make us recognize this common bond."

In the 1988 article, "Ronald Reagan's Obsession with an Alien Invasion," A. Hovni wrote:

"Gorbachev himself confirmed the conversation in Geneva during an important speech on February 17, 1987, in the Grand Kremlin Palace in Moscow, to the Central Committee of the USSR's Communist Party. Gorbachev was further quoted as saying:

At our meeting in Geneva, the U.S. President said that if the earth faced an invasion by extra-terrestrials, the United States and the Soviet Union would join forces to repel such an invasion. I shall not dispute the hypothesis, though I think it's early yet to worry about such an intrusion...."

It is interesting to point out that Gorbachev never spoke of how weird the conversation was; he only commented that it may be too early to talk about such an event as an alien invasion. Did this indicate that perhaps there is a date when it would be more appropriate to discuss these things? Or have the governments of the world been planning on a date where they announce to the world that "life is out there in space" — or have they been planning on a date where they would stage an alien invasion?

On December 7th, 2012 Russian prime minister Medvedev during an on-camera interview with reporters in Moscow, continued to respond to reporters and made some off-air comments without realizing that his microphone was still on. He was then asked by one reporter if "the president is handed secret files on aliens when he receives the briefcase needed to activate Russia's nuclear arsenal." Medvedev responded: Along with the briefcase with nuclear codes, the president of the country is given a special 'top secret' folder. This folder in its entirety contains information about aliens who visited our planet... Along with this, you are given a report of the absolutely secret special service that exercises control over aliens on the territory of our country... More detailed information on this topic you can get from a well-known movie called Men In Black... I will not tell you how many of them are among us because it may cause panic.

Western news sources reporting on Medvedev's shocking reply about aliens stated that he was "joking" as he mentioned the movie *Men in Black*, which they wrongly assumed was a reference to the 1997 American sci-fi adventure comedy about two top secret agents battling aliens in the US.

Medvedev, however, wasn't referring to the American movie but was, instead, talking about the famous Russian movie documentary *Men in Black* which details many UFO and alien anomalies.

Where Western news sources quoted Medvedev as saying "More detailed information on this topic you can get from a well-known movie called *Men In Black*,'" his actual answer was, "You can receive more detailed information having watched the documentary film of the same name."

The reason(s) for Western propaganda news outlets deliberately distorting Medvedev's words become apparent after his shocking statement, and as evidenced in just one example of their so called reporting on this disclosure of alien life already being on our planet where the title of one such article was "Russian Prime Minister Dmitri Medvedev makes a crack about aliens, and conspiritists promptly lose their minds."

There was also some commotion in 2014 when the honorable Canadian minister of defense Paul Helleyer claimed that the United States are working with at least 4 types of aliens and that a Synarchy exists in the

U.S. as he claimed government leaders are in touch with what he called "the tall whites."

On February 12th, 2014, outgoing senior Obama adviser John Podesta reflected on his latest White House stint, listing his favorite moments and biggest regrets from the past year. Chief among them: depriving the American people of the truth about UFOs.

Podesta's longtime fascination with UFOs is well-documented, as his brief political hiatus following four years as President Bill Clinton's Chief of Staff freed him up to pursue his otherworldly passion.

At a 2002 press conference organized by the Coalition for Freedom of Information, Podesta spoke on the importance of disclosing government UFO investigations to the public.

On Friday the 13th, 2014 Podesta tweeted his regret about the nondisclosure of UFOs and *The Washington Post* immediately recalled an exchange one of its reporters had with Podesta in 2007. Karen Tumulty had asked Podesta about reports that the Clinton Library in Little Rock, Arkansas had been bombarded with Freedom of Information Act Requests specifically seeking email correspondence to and from the former chief of staff including terms like "X-Files" and "Area 51." Podesta's response, through a spokesperson, was "The truth is out there," the tagline for the TV show "The X-Files," of which Podesta was known to be a fan.

A 2010 editorial in Missouri's *Columbia Tribune* disparaged reports that Podesta had asked an outspoken UFO photographer to stop discussing his knowledge of extraterrestrial activities in public.

"One wonders why Podesta would do such a radical reversal, given his former plea for UFO disclosure," the editorial implored.

But contrary to the *Columbia Tribune*'s concerns, Podesta had clearly not abandoned the cause. He wrote an introduction to the 2010 book *UFOs: Generals, Pilots, and Government Officials Go on the Record*, by Leslie Kean. Unfortunately, Podesta will likely have little time to fill out FOIA requests in his new job at Hillary Clinton's presidential campaign.

However, Bill Clinton also reflected the same attitude Ronald Reagan had about UFOs and confirmed Podesta's reports when he appeared on Jimmy Kimmel Live.

After all of the new information that is out there, all of the data dumps and statements' by officials. From Truman to Eisenhower to other presidents that have been upfront about UFOs what more evidence do you need that this phenomenon is real and that the alien disclosure was made at various times throughout history?

It seems that the information is now blatant and that there are most certainly unknown aerial phenomena that needs to be discovered and reported.

SILENT WEAPONS FOR SILENT WARS

X-FILES: SILENT WEAPONS FOR SILENT WARS

"There is a Power so organized, so subtle, so complete, so pervasive, that had better not speak, above their breath when they speak in condemnation of it." -- President Woodrow Wilson

There are times when I freak out over discoveries I make, and there are times when those I associate with, who continually tell me that I have completely lost it, start agreeing with me that something is just not right. This is when I start to worry. I think that either I am doing a good job of convincing them, or they are making their own personal discoveries. The last thing that I wrote was a 10-page manuscript that tried to explain the movie X-files: Fight the future. Like Charles Fort admonishes one cannot measure a circle from anywhere. Once you find the answers more questions come up. Such was the case when I received a phone call from an office friend Helen, telling me that a very important newscaster, whom I respect, Rod Decker called. He wanted to talk with me about something. My last interview with Decker was a sham. It wasn't Decker's fault. It was after the Heaven's Gate Suicides.

He wanted to interview me, two members of the Band Dharma Combat, UFO Contactee Victoria Lillijenquist, and a University of Utah Professor about UFOs. Well it turned into a Circus, and I wasn't about to join in because obviously, the professor had his agenda, Victoria had to prove herself, the Band members were lamenting the loss of their fellow band mate who was one of the 39 found dead in rancho Santa Fe and I just watched in disbelief. The professor did exactly what he was supposed to do. Objectively point out that not every light we see in the sky is a UFO, or an extraterrestrial craft. I agreed with him. However, there was overwhelming evidence to show that what is going on needs to be investigated. I never had a chance to say it. That was 1997.

In 1998 things are changing once again and attitudes are changing as well. Scientists at Stanford University have agreed to investigate the phenomena. This is why Rod Decker wanted to speak with me. When the Washington Post reports UFOs, it must be real. Then and only then do I get an interview. Don't get me wrong, I am looking forward to this, but I am frustrated that for 3 years I have tried to talk objectively about this phenomenon, and have been ignored by my hometown media. UFOs are still "side show " materials, like the Bearded Lady, or the Lobster Boy at a carnival. One Colleague of mine who is an excellent reporter for the paranormal was told by his superiors not to report such nonsense. The official stance by his paper is that these reports are fabrications. They are dead wrong. Some of the stories could be falsehoods, but in an even peculiar way that still warrants an investigation. I am now going to toot my horn, I am right. You as a reader and listener are right, for taking the time to investigate. They are wrong.

I had talked with Kevin Hill, who is a listener to Ground Zero and a part time writer for Disinfozero and he made a very interesting observation. One that made me very happy. He observed that Ground Zero is not just my work. But it is everyone who has the time to stop and investigate what is going on in a world gone out of control. I agree with him. I have stressed many times that it is your own empowerment that gives you the truth. My beliefs do not reign supreme. I am merely the voice. The messenger. I am here to forewarn of what might be. Together we need to fight against the silent war. There are many others out there who attempt to do the same. While some are just cheerleaders for an entertaining freak show. I am bound and determined to learn as much as I can. This will protect me, and hopefully you from a future that may be controlled by a small group of individuals who want to use fear and violence to enslave us. It's a quiet war. The weapons don't pop or explode. They confuse. They are armed. Are you?

Using Knowledge as a defense against the controlling media is a war that has been going on for an undetermined period of time. Taking Consensus reality and changing it takes time. The truth usually wins. Stories buzz past you and some are outrageous, and some are believable, you utilize faith and hope you are not wrong. A Survey published in George magazine polled 800 American adults. The poll revealed that 3 out of four citizens in that sample believe that the U.S. Government is involved in clandestine, conspiratorial operations. This is not a fantasy. This is reality. The Government isn't the only group that has a exclusive possession of distrust. We are distrusting everything. People do not trust people. It's not just the criminal element that has the distrust of the people. Political leaders, clergyman, and self appointed experts are all suspect. Which brings us full circle to the X-files movie. Here is a piece of Fiction that if you investigate it, has a cryptic message to it. Granted I have covered this ground before, but little did I know that there was more to the Puzzle.

I just couldn't get out of my head the images and the words that were being thrown around in the movie X-files: Fight the Future. Forgive me for being obsessive but there are things you need to know about what was said in the film.

First of all Dr. Alvin Kurtsweil Mulder's contact in the bar is a fictitious character. Dr. Stephen Kursweil is not. Now you know why I am obsessed. Dr. Kursweil had a run in with someone who I had met in Roswell New Mexico in 1997. Bud Hopkins. Bud has been involved in the hypnosis of abductees. Getting them to recall their abduction for the benefit of assessment. I happen to know two of his patients. They told me that Bud was a kind man, and from what I could tell he was concerned about these abduction cases and spoke at a gathering during the 50th anniversary of the Roswell Crash. Dr. Kursweil however, has a different perspective.

Kursweil allegedly was introduced to Bud Hopkins by a CIA operative during a MUFON meeting in Boston. Kursweil in a sworn affidavit claims that Hopkins worked for the CIA as well, and that his hypnosis techniques were causing problems with the patients. He claimed that Hopkins said that the CIA was worried about the abduction claims. The CIA was curious if these subjects were being programmed. Kursweil was alarmed at the suicide rate of these abductees and thought that what Hopkins was doing was barbaric to people already in distress. Kursweil reported Hopkins to medical authorities. Kursweil claims that Hopkins returned the favor and reported him as being delusional and paranoid about a government cover up.

What this shows is a virtual Pissing match between two people who are in the UFO fraternity. The coincidences with the names of Kurtsweil and Kursweil are even more fortuitous, when you take a look at the back pages of the book "Behold a Pale Horse" by William Cooper. The whole account is there in black and white. It also becomes highly likely that William Cooper's theories and stories may have been the inspiration for the movie X-files fight the Future. Chapter 1 of the book is entitled "Silent weapons for Quiet wars." Not only does Martin Landau use the quote "Silent weapons for a quiet war" in the movie, but also on page 121 of the book the story of the secret government FEMA unfolds. The beginning chapter greets us with PATRIOTS and TAX PROTESTERS: YOU MUST NEVER BE FOUND AT HOME ON ANY HOLIDAY! YOUR LIFE DEPENDS ON HOW WELL YOU CAN OBEY THAT RULE. Landau's character Kurtsweil tells Mulder that the plague will be unleashed on a Holiday and that FEMA; the Federal Emergency Management Agency will declare a state of emergency empowering them to suspend the constitution.

What is the protocol for such a declaration? Something as simple suspension of debt payments by high bureaus of American Countries, to mass runs on U.S. commercial banks, to food shortages, to drug wars, to instability in the Middle east. This Executive Order is numbered 11051. It gives Authorization to put all executive orders into effect in times of national emergency declared by the President. The order does not mention war or nuclear attack. It does mention increased international tensions, economical or financial crisis. But that is not all. There were a number of other executive orders that would allow FEMA to takeover, communications, utilities, food resources, and all modes of transportation. Also there is that dirty little executive order that states that the postmaster general can operate an emergency registration of all persons. And that the Housing and Finance authority can relocate communities, designate areas that are off limits, and establish new locations for the populace, Such as the dreaded Concentration Camp Bunkers set aside for subversives who do not cooperate with Law enforcement. President Richard M. Nixon combined these orders into one big order. All power would be turned over to the head of FEMA. In case of a National emergency. This in turn was again proposed as Executive order 11490 and was signed by President Jimmy Carter on

July 20th, 1979. It is in fact the Law. If we were in a national Crisis a state of Anarchy would ensue. You would not know whom to trust.

Mulder tells Kurtsweil that he is full of shit. Kurtsweil laughs and let's Mulder investigate for himself the truth about the "Quiet War." That a disease will be unleashed to an ignorant populace, causing a state of emergency. Then soon after the New Government will be put into place the Federal Emergency Management Agency. The disease is an extra terrestrial plague far more devastating than Aids or E-bola. An insect, in the movie's case an Africanized Honeybee will transport the disease.

Reality is stranger than fiction once again. While ground has been covered in a previous article, there is another case that is far more curious, than the Killer bee scare in Texas. Between 1956-1958, the U.S. Army conducted field experiments in Savanna Georgia, and Avon Park Florida using Mosquitoes. They were released in residential areas. Many people were swarmed and many people became sick and died as a result of the bites. The details of the experiment are classified, however some claim that the victims died of yellow fever.

A Story published in the LA times, September 26th 1990 reported that the AIDS Virus is attacking more children than previously thought. It was reported then that 10 million children would be afflicted with the disease by the year 2000. Also in 1990 it was reported that 400,000 cases or a third of the 1.2 million estimated cases of AIDS worldwide were believed to have occurred in children under the age of 5. Now keep in mind that 400,000 children are not homosexual. 400,000 children are not IV Drug users, or that 400,000 or 1/3 of their mothers have transmitted the disease. Did some of them get the disease by other methods? If so, could one of those methods be by insect? It is only a question, With no answer. However it could be.

In the film, the syndicate, or secret organization has a vaccine. This vaccine is used to prevent the disease from mutating in the human body. This mutation eventually turns into a gestating extraterrestrial biological entity that feeds on human flesh for survival. Those who have the vaccine would be able to have control over the populace. Kurtsweil says in the film, that the secret cult of intelligence has been developing this vaccine for at least 50 years. That they have been providing hosts for these ancient aliens for some time now, in exchange for power.

William Cooper once again comes into play for this bit of alleged truth. He claims that he personally saw papers about an alliance between our government and an alien race.

In the film the "Secret meeting" in London reveals that this alliance has been broken by the aliens. Cooper once again can be connected with the same story. He claims that those aliens have broken deals, but our government cannot stop them because they have better weapons than we do. Cooper also states that Alien scientists are behind Cattle Mutilations and human abductions. Cooper has gone as far as to classify the aliens that come and go on this planet:

- The classic Grey.
- The ones in abduction stories.
- A Big nosed Grey
- Tall Blonde Nordic aliens
- Orange skinned aliens

The classic moment in the movie is when Scully tells Mulder that she has decided to transfer to Salt Lake City, Utah. It is then she is rushed to the hospital after she falls victim to a Killer Bee sting containing the Alien organism. Mulder calls 911. An ambulance arrives and they take her away. However the driver of the ambulance is a part of the conspiracy and shoots Mulder in the head. As the ambulance drives off into the shadows, the movie throws us a hint as to who may be behind all of this wonderful conspiracy theory. The doors of the ambulance have printed in huge block letters COOPER.

The mystery does not cease with the film. The soundtrack has many cryptic puzzle pieces as well. Track 14 on the X-files Soundtrack has a special message recorded from Chris Carter himself. The message begins when track 14 has hit 10:13. Ten Thirteen Productions is his production company. However it is still unclear if Carter has taken a clue from Robert Anton Wilson. The dark coincidences attributed to the number 23 can be applied to 10:13.
10+13=23.

One last coincidence is quite pleasant and brings us full circle again. In the beginning of the movie we learn that the X-files have been closed. Through the labors of Scully and Mulder we see that the X-files are reopened after an overwhelming amount of evidence points to a sinister plot to transport an alien disease around the world. Within days of the X-files release to theaters, It was announced that scientists have decided that there is overwhelming evidence to warrant a full-scale investigation into UFO phenomena. This is the first time in 30 years that anyone has formally decided to take on such a responsibility.

Believe me I know the difference between fact and fiction. However lately we see such a gray line between what is real and what is above reality. How is it that in a time when information is at the click of a button, that we can become so confused? So full of mistrust?

Maybe it's because all of the propaganda doesn't sell the lie like it used to. Maybe the lie has to be so outrageous, that it clouds the true evil that hides in the shadows. We need to read between the lines. No one is going to come right out and say it. I mean that would make them a paranoid conspiracy freak, and we all know that there is no such thing as a conspiracy right?

SECURITY MATTER X

As I have been digging deeper into the history of the UFO era and it's connect ions to the Northwest, I remember the first X-files episode and it too began in the Northwest with a series of abduction cases. Agent Dana Scully and Fox Mulder have to fly to Oregon to investigate the occurrences which my opinion gives a nod to the rich history of intrigue and conspiracy that has its roots in the Northwest.

On June 21, 1947, the beginnings of the cold war UFO era began when it was reported that six unidentified flying objects were seen in the skies over Maury Island, situated near Tacoma in Puget Sound area of Washington State. The recorded eyewitnesses to the incident were Harbor patrolman Harold A. Dahl who was piloting a boat in the bay, his two crewmen, his teenage son and a dog.

The UFO's were doughnut-shaped and were seen hovering over the boat. They were reported to be about 2000 miles up and one of the six craft looked like it was in trouble. It began losing altitude and was being circled by the other five. Each of the objects were estimated to be about one hundred feet in diameter.

The disc that was having trouble suffered an explosion and spewed hot metal in to the air. Some of the hot metal or "slag" hit the boat, killing the Dahl's dog, damaging the boat and injuring the teenage son. Dahl began taking pictures of the objects, which soon took off. He claimed that the craft were heading towards Canada. Dahl radioed for help but the radio was having trouble getting any message out to anyone. He decided to head to land back to the city of Tacoma. He rushed his son to the hospital to have his burns treated.

He decided to speak to his boss about the incident. He grabbed the slag samples and his camera and spoke to Fred Lee Crisman. It turns out that Crisman was a very interesting man and for years his name would be spoken of by Conspiracy theorists for some time.

Crisman had wanted to investigate Dahl's claims but Dahl apparently had been warned off by what could be described as a Man in Black or G-man. No one except Dahl or Crisman knew that the incident had happened and so it was rather odd that this strange man showed up and warned to avoid the incident and to forget it ever took place.

Undaunted, Crisman finally returned to Maury island only to find some broken glass and what appeared to be thin metal. He also claimed that he saw another flying machine but the case was only a small town incident and really didn't gain any momentum, authorities had hoped that it would be forgotten.

Then comes the big news story of pilot Kenneth Arnold and his sighting of strange craft flying over Mount Rainer. This begins to kick the Flying saucer story full throttle and the United States begins to see these flying saucers everywhere.

Kenneth Arnold arranges to meet Harold Dahl in Tacoma, Washington at the request of Raymond Palmer who is a pulp fiction writer and friend of Fred Crisman. Palmer is well remembered as the man responsible for the magazines, "Amazing Stories," and "FATE" and wants to give a 200 dollar advance on the story of the Northwest UFO's. Arnold goes to Tacoma to meet with Dahl but finds out that all of the Hotels there are booked. He then finds out that there is a Hotel room booked in his name at a fancy hotel in town. The room is booked by someone anonymously.

He finally meets up with Dahl. However Dahl becomes a bit paranoid because he claims that the man in Black frightened him and told him not to speak with anyone. However Arnold is motivated by the Cash Advance and wants the story so he presses Dahl for more information on the Incident.

Dahl had no evidence of the encounter, didn't have photos or anything else, just a piece of rock that he claimed fell from the Flying donut object.

Dahl then claims that he also received a letter stating that the objects he saw were piloted by alien beings that have decided to show themselves now that we have been using atomic weapons.

The question is who wrote the letter? Many believe it was Crisman.

The entire transcript of their discussion winds up on the desks of the editors of United press International. It was all becoming clear – someone was targeting Arnold, booked him a room, bugged it, and had the story.

There was an all out attempt to discredit the story – for reasons no one could fathom.

Turned out the Crisman was part of the OSS the group that existed prior to the CIA and was also involved with Operation paper clip, where German scientists were filtered in after World War II to work on secret space programs, bombs and some people believe secret saucer technology.

Crisman knew too much, however at the time he seemed to be the observer watching every part of the UFO lore fall into place.
Kenneth Arnold was debriefed by the Military and did an Interview with Ted Smith on radio station KWRC in Pendleton. He decided that he would turn over some of the evidence form Maury Island to Lieutenant Brown and Captain Davidson. They agreed to fly out to Tacoma immediately to see what Arnold had. It was rumored that someone had already tipped them off that the event was a hoax; however they flew out anyway.

At the airport, Crisman, the man the intelligence officers seemed to think was lying, turned up and gave the men a box which he said was filled with the slag from the damaged UFO. Arnold thought that all that was in the box was rocks. The men stowed the box in the trunk of their car and left for the airport, catching their flight.

They were killed in route as their B-25 plane crashed somewhere in Kelso Washington. What was really in that box?

It was a week later the Roswell Crash happened and the world was awakened to the possibility of a flying disc crash and the rest is history. On July 11th, 1947 another flying disc crash was reported from Fort Douglas Utah, the Disc crash was in Idaho and was investigated by known FBI asset William Guy Bannister. Bannister was a resident of Idaho and worked out the FBI office in Montana.

He was the man in charge of investigating all UFO cases in the west and northwest.

Declassified FBI files from 1947 show a number of telexes initialed WGB , all pertained to UFO phenomena, they had the designation 'Security Matter -X' or simply 'SM-X,' – could it be that the FBI did have an X-files and that they were being headed up by Banister? Was he the Man In Black that warned off Dahl and did he know Crisman?

Coincidentally both men were implicated in the JFK assassination.
On the afternoon of November 22, 1963, the day that President John F. Kennedy was assassinated, Banister and one of his investigators, Jack Martin, were drinking together at the Katzenjammer Bar, located next

door to 544 Camp Street, New Orleans. On their return to Banister's office, the two men got into a dispute. Banister believed that Martin had stolen some files and drew his .357 magnum revolver, striking Martin with it several times. During the altercation Martin yelled: "What are you going to do — kill me like you all did Kennedy?" Martin was badly injured and treated at Charity Hospital.

Over the next few days, Martin told authorities and reporters that Banister and anti-Castro activist David Ferrie had been involved in the assassination. He claimed that Ferrie knew Oswald from their days in the New Orelan Civil Air patrol, and that Ferrie might have taught Oswald how to use a rifle with a telescopic sight. Martin also claimed that Banister had often been in the company of Ferrie, and that Ferrie drove to Texas on the day of Kennedy's assassination, to serve as a getaway pilot for the assassins

Now in a great coincidence Fred Crisman was one of the three tramps arrested in Dallas immediately after JFK's assassination. Many people believe that Crisman was the gunman on the Grassy Knoll.

Crisman is also named in New Orleans District Attorney Jim Garrison's 1968 investigation into the Kennedy assassination, in which Garrison maintained that Crisman may have been an assassin working on behalf of aerospace concerns to kill Kennedy.

The loose ends of this whole case have been tied together by Investigator Kenn Thomas who is the noted authority on the connections of the UFO's of the Northwest, the Man In Black, Banister and the go between alleged CIA asset Crisman.

Thomas has said that most of his evidence comes from declassified documents said that one of the recently surfaced MJ12 documents suggests that Crisman turned samples of the debris over to Clay Shaw, one of the three people that Garrison attempted to indict in the alleged conspiracy to kill Kennedy.

Shaw was acquitted of any wrong doing but he also was a CIA operative. One of the strange twists about Crisman that is never explained is that his strange connection to Ray Palmer. He had written many short stories about his encounters with underground beings called the DEROS. Chrisman's accounts were similar to the reports of the modern known alien grays. The creatures mostly noted in the Betty and Barney Hill case and the Communion books written by Whitley Strieber. Crisman had claimed that during World War II he fought the DEROS in caverns located in Burma.

The case has many twists and turns and when examined is only part of the complicated mosaic that is the modern UFO phenomenon

A CURIOUS AQUARIUS

A few weeks ago we presented exclusive information about the Maury island incident at the McMinnville UFO festival. The Maury Island incident has been literally censored by the United States Military and it also has been called a hoax in some UFO circles. I have always wondered why this case has been kept under wraps and the more I investigate the more I am realizing that this incident is most definitely the key in understanding what happened back in the 1940's and how many incidents that happened before Roswell indicate a very real cover up and conspiracy that has many tentacles.

Sir Francis Bacon wrote; "All Governments are obscure and invisible." This seems to apply to a shadow government that has many secrets and how much of what was once secret is most certainly being discovered and there are dots that need to be connected in order to bring the truth into the sunlight.

You may remember that when we covered Maury Island and when we did research in the Tacoma, Washington archives, we were able to connect Maury island witness Fred Crisman with Clay Shaw. Clay Shaw of course was prosecuted by New Orleans District Attorney Jim Garrison for his alleged role in the JFK assassination.

Shaw was most certainly an established CIA contract agent. The truth about what he did with the CIA is even more interesting. Shaw had admitted working with the OSS and was involved with the pipelining of German scientists to the United States under Project paperclip. Now, these scientists were Nazi war criminals and had a secret that they carried with them and that is the secret of space and rocket technology. Many of these scientists admitted that much of what they were working on at war's end was secret technology provided by other worldly entities that they claimed were Aryan secret rulers.

It was 1947 and the secret Nazi collusion had been cemented in secret and the UFO sightings were becoming more and more prevalent. This was no accident and it looked as if Fred Lee Crisman's connection to the events at Maury Island were not a coincidence.

Crisman not only worked with Shaw during 'Project Paperclip,' but also was involved with security at Boeing and other aerospace companies after the World War II. Crisman gave his story of a saucer fleet that was in trouble and the saucer that spewed hot metal on to his boat. Crisman gave samples of what he called slag to *"two army G-2 intelligence officers."*

G-2 was very interested in any and all early flying saucer reports, but it also was their responsibility to keep a tight lid on Project Paperclip. The slag was classified material and it was placed along with other UFO pieces in a box and then loaded on to a B-25 aircraft. The plane exploded and crashed in a wooded area near Kelso, Washington.

Three days after the Maury Island affair Kenneth Arnold's sighting of nine silver craft in the same area of the United States kicked off the "Flying saucer "craze. Since 1947 there has been speculation and hypothesis about why the United States has been involved with the cover-up and now nearly 70 years later there are now documents becoming declassified and evidence that suggests that the technology that has been considered otherworldly has been reverse engineered and is being used by our military today.

There are also uncovered documents which also indicate that since the 1940's (around the time of Maury Island and The Kenneth Arnold sightings) where we began to see an intelligence split from the OSS to the CIA and NSA, that there has been a spook war between a CIA group known as Aquarius and Com-12.

There have been several other so-called shadow groups that have not been named and their services are classified under extra intelligence "command." These agencies allegedly have more power than the executive and act without congressional oversight.

On May 21st, 2014, Dr. Steven Greer announced that his Disclosure group "received a cache of Top Secret documents related to "Project Aquarius", a purported Majestic 12 (MJ-12) covert project related to UFOs/ETs. Previously, summaries of the documents have appeared on the Internet. However, we received photos of the actual documents."
I immediately contacted Dr. Greer's people for comment and they have replied to our inquiry about the documents and we hope to get some more information as it comes in. In the meantime, we have been able to look over the documents as he and his team have been able to make them available to the press.

According to Greer's website he claims that, "The person who sent us these documents has numerous legitimate contacts in covert aerospace and military projects related to UFOs and is a credible and reliable source."

We also are in contact with an aerospace source and will provide you with more information as it becomes available to us.

Meanwhile, there have been some amazing events that have transpired in the last few days that are worthy of reporting that are quite mysterious and compelling.

As far back as 2007 a phenomenon known as "fast radio bursts" or FRBs have left astronomers wondering about the possibility that there has been a lot of collisions of neutron stars or if the signals are part of some extraterrestrial communication.

The light signals occur for several milliseconds and come out of nowhere. Back in 2007, the bursts were actually intermittent and minimal, now the burst are happening at a quicker pace which could mean that this is some kind of communication.

On May 27th, 2014 Ground Zero reported:

On May 21st, 2014, an event happened where highly critical scientists that have since been very skeptical of the extra-terrestrial question have now become more open to the possibility. The US House of Representatives Committee on Science, Space, and Technology heard from Seth Shostak and Dan Werthimer, who both direct Berkeley's new 'Search for Extra-Terrestrial Intelligence' or SETI.

As Nature News World reported in their article, 'Congress Hears About the Hunt For Alien Life', "*Werthimer introduced the committee to his institute's work by explaining that their main goal is to answer the question "Is anybody out there?" ... Werthimer told the committee that if there is, they will find it, as the institute stays focused on searching for signs of life in the galaxy primarily among planets with the telltale signs of oxygen or methane gases – which have been commonly associated with life.*"

Seth Shostak, Senior Astronomer with SETI, says that the evidence of extra-terrestrial life will most definitely be revealed within 10-20 years. Nature News continued by saying, "*Shostak also introduced the congressmen to a long-running project that involves the search for signals intentionally sent out by other civilizations equally curious in their own search for life.*"

In her article 'Astronomers Baffled By Mystery Rasio Bursts From Space,' Gabrielle Pickard wrote for TopSecretWriters.com and said:

"In April this year, the latest rapid frequency bursts were sighted; their explanation still remains unknown. That has, however, not stopped people from speculating what the mysterious pulsing signals could be. Theories include the light being caused by colliding neutron stars and, predictably, that aliens are trying to make contact with us.

Due to the fact FRB's occur sporadically and temporarily, these radio emissions are not only difficult to find but they are almost impossible to study.

It was in 2007 when the first FRB was picked up by radio telescopes. The temporary nature of the radio messages meant it took time for scientists to even agree that the signal wasn't caused by a glitch in one of the telescope's instruments. The signal lasted for just five milliseconds. It was named the Lorimer Burst after Duncan Lorimer, an astrophysicist at West Virginia University in Morgantown who made the discovery."

It is interesting to note that as this report was being prepared the Pope allegedly made his statements about not being alone in the Universe. It was reported in several Italian newspapers that the Pope made this statement during a homily just days after the Easter mass.

The question is whether or not that Vatican was aware of these fast radio bursts and is SETI also aware of these bursts and is this why they tell us that communication with extra terrestrials is closer than we once thought?

In the meantime, some compelling UFO footage has been produced out of Puerto Rico. The security cameras on surveillance helicopters picked up two very fast moving objects with night vision.

In April of 2013 infrared cameras picked up on two UFO's flying over Aguadilla. The footage is amazing and it is not clear as to what the aircraft are, but as we say in the business timing is everything and as we see there have been a number of curious things that have happened all leading up to possible disclosure the declassification of documents that prove that there has been an investigation into UFO's codenamed Aquarius.

The Aquarius/CIA connections go all the way back to Maury island and I am sure that if we dig deep enough we could find intelligence linking the Nazis to the space technology provided by other worldly sources.
This would mean that there could be a war of minds with old-school Aquarius/CIA agents pitted against Command 12 agents. This, once again, indicates an octopus of agencies inextricably entangled in one of the greatest cover ups in our history.

The old stories that have been censored and declared hoaxes are actually valuable stories that connect the intelligence agencies of the government with the aerospace agencies that are responsible for secret aircraft and possible collusion with so-called extra-terrestrials that provided Nazi scientist with information on propulsion engines that would bring the entire space program and military industrial complex into the spotlight with regard to the alien question. To me there is no question and the more we unravel this case the closer we will get to the truth.

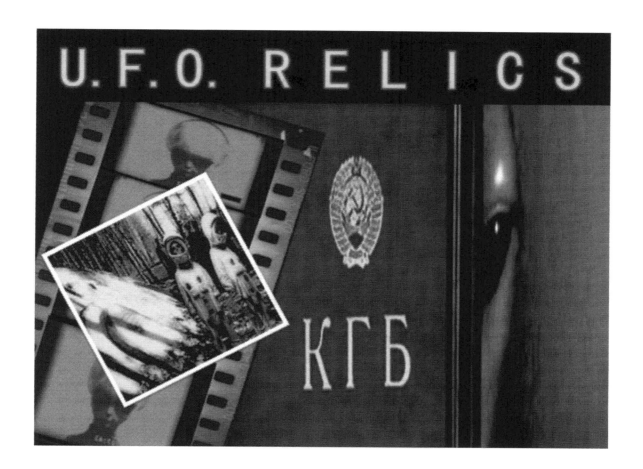

U.F.O. RELICS

It was just before Christmas when I caught a story out of Russia confirming a strange story that I had previously written off as an elaborate hoax. The state radio broadcast of 'The Voice of Russia' made a strange announcement about a KGB secret file that was declassified. The file was regarding a UFO incident that took place in 1969 and was the subject of an elaborate TNT network special that was hosted by Roger Moore.

In 1998, the television program 'The Secret KGB UFO Files,' purported to show startling film segments of a crashed saucer surrounded by Russian soldiers, as well as footage of what appeared to be an autopsy of an alleged alien torso and an apparent dead alien.

Skeptics pored over the footage and concluded that it was a well-produced fake for TNT. A lot of what was shown were allegedly reenactments and not 'black market' footage as first reported.

One of the biggest debunkers of the incident was James Oberg who is well-known for being a debunker of anything alien and/or UFO.

While it may be that the television show had produced very convincing footage – to the point of not being believed – the Voice of Russia, which currently broadcasts to 109 million listeners in 160 countries and is considered one of the top five radio broadcasters in the world, is now circulating the story as fact.

In 1969, in the state of Sverdlovsky, a UFO was reported to have crashed and was recovered by the Russian military. *"There was film that allegedly showed the recovery of a saucer. There was one dead alien found in the craft. The remains of the alien and the UFO debris were taken to a secure Russian site, where the saucer was analyzed, and an autopsy was done on the alien."*

The Huffington Post wrote: *"The Voice of Russia also includes references to unconfirmed reports that a UFO crashed or was shot down near the city of Prohlandnyi, in the USSR on Aug. 10, 1989. Like the previous story, this one included alleged alien bodies."*

I sat on this story throughout the holiday wondering if there would come a time when it would become more relevant.

The Huffington Post and several other mainstream outlets jumped on to the story and placed it in its "odd file," only to be forgotten or doubted. I was puzzled as to why this story has returned and why it has now received the blessing of the "state radio" of Russia as being real and that Russia now is beginning to loosen its intelligence on UFO's and contact with alien civilizations.

The U.S. media has taken a loathing of UFO stories and hasn't paid much attention to them. It is as if UFO – and possible alien related stories – have now been placed into the category of 'hoax' until proven otherwise, which has placed UFO observation in the same category as having imaginary friends.

The fact is, UFO stories are ubiquitous and not just relics of the Cold War. The problem with any UFO story that is generated now is the tendency of the court of public opinion to assume that all UFO reports are about aliens and or other new age free energy topics which create a schism where scientists wish to stay clear of.

It can also be said that Russian and American UFOlogy has been compromised because it is difficult to ascertain which UFO reports are the product of secret Soviet and American space and military experiments.

However, it is my opinion that *this is* what makes UFOlogy fascinating. As more documents become declassified, it is quite telling as to what can be identified and what seems to be considered unexplained. The more we are exposed to the declassification of some documents from the KGB and other government intelligence agencies, the more we realize that most governments are now – or have been aware for some time – that extra-terrestrial craft have either shown up here on Earth or have been observed and have crashed.

It should be noted that Russian Prime Minister Dmitry Medvedev remarked in 2012, that, as Collective-Evolution.com wrote, *"the president receives classified information on extraterrestrials visiting the planet at the beginning of his term."*

It is also important to remember the conversation former United States president Ronald Reagan had with Russian President Mikhail Gorbachev in Geneva about the possible threat of extra-terrestrials in the near future.

In the 1988 article, 'Ronald Reagan's Obsession With An Alien Invasion', A. Hovni wrote that, *"Gorbachev himself confirmed the conversation in Geneva during an important speech on February 17, 1987, in the Grand Kremlin Palace in Moscow, to the Central Committee of the USSR's Communist Party."*

Gorbachev stated, *"At our meeting in Geneva, the U.S. President said that if the earth faced an invasion by extra-terrestrials, the United States and the Soviet Union would join forces to repel such an invasion. I shall not dispute the hypothesis, though I think it's early yet to worry about such an intrusion..."*

It is interesting to point out that Gorbachev never spoke of how weird the conversation was; he only commented that it may be too early to talk about such an event as an alien invasion. Did this indicate that perhaps there is a date when it would be more appropriate to discuss these things? Or have the governments of the world been planning on a date where they announce to the world that 'life is out there in space' – or have they been planning on a date where they would stage an alien invasion?

This would further the argument that UFOlogists have spoken of for a long time and that is a "black budget" that is set aside for a the very real threats from space and that includes the possibility of hostile alien species.

There is always a debate as to whether or not an extraterrestrial threat is real or that the government is capable of manufacturing a worldwide hoax in order to secure the establishment of a one world power.

Ronald Reagan had expressed that the differences of the planet would be neutralized if it were revealed that world threat existed and that the threat would be extra terrestrial.

Last August, Edward Snowden blew the whistle on the surveillance state, but he also disclosed some other interesting things with regard to black budgets that are set aside for unknown reasons.

Many have speculated that these budgets are for aviation and space vehicles for defense.

When Snowden sought asylum in Venezuela, he actually spoke about UFO's and allegedly said, *"As it turns out, the most credible and inexplicable sightings are of vehicles which have been spotted leaving the sea floor at hydrothermal vents and directly entering solar orbit."*
This would make the argument that what we are dealing with are ultra-terrestrial vehicles that are capable of hiding in the ocean and in space.

Again, Collective-Evolution.com writes, "*Former National Minister of Defence for Canada, Paul Hellyer alluded to trillions of dollars going into black budget projects in which congress and the president are deliberately kept in the dark. The secret seems to be exploding out even more as we head towards 2014.*"

You may remember that during a Ground Zero broadcast, our program was cut off after a listener phoned in to speak about Hellyer's comments during the Citizen hearing on disclosure about an alien group called "The Tall Whites."

Tall, frail beings are allegedly involved with government decisions according to Hellyer and according to him there are some that were seen at a base in Nevada.

While the "tall whites" maybe considered a tall tale by some, the reality is that while we discussed the issue on the air, our satellite hookup was shut down during our "Mortgiest" broadcast and immediately a back-up show was broadcast in its place.

Meanwhile, the UFO-themed stories were suddenly becoming mainstream as ABC reported a UFO flap over California and the United Kingdom reported a UFO the size of a rugby ball buzzed a commercial aircraft over Heathrow Airport.

Peter Davenport, who is the director of the National UFO Reporting Center, says that there has been a lot of UFO sightings lately. He stated to me that he took about a month's worth of UFO sightings in one night. Federal authorities have stated that there has been no unusual flight activity in California; however, a rash of UFO reports beginning the morning of New Year's Day from Sacramento to Auburn.

Meanwhile, the UK reports a near miss with an A320 aircraft at 34,000 feet back in July. The pilot told investigators that the object passed within a few feet of the top of the jet and that it was "cigar or rugby ball-like" in shape, bright silver and "metallic" in construction.

The publication of the report was released to the press on January 6th, 2013.

Nick Pope, who was a former Ministry of Defense and UFO investigator, appeared on Ground Zero in May 2013. He reported that the UFO investigations in the U.K. were closed in 2009. However, this did not stop the sightings and the reports as the Civil Aviation Authority made the decision to look into reports being provided by air crew and air traffic controllers.

In 2012, it was announced that despite the fact that the MOD ceased its interest in UFO reports the National Air Traffic Control services claimed that there would be a report of a UFO every month.

Meanwhile, Russia is continuing its ongoing openness about its UFO history. There are reports that declassified documents confirm that Russia's first contact with extraterrestrials happened in 1942.
It must be stressed that the so-called "little green men" mentality does not exist in Russia. The KGB was never at liberty to disclose anything to its citizenry and up until now has kept a tight lid on anything this strange.

However, as the state media begins the task of revealing – little by little – the UFO cases in Russia, imaginations are running wild and the UFO excitement that existed in the 1970's through 1990's in the United States has taken hold in Russia.

In the United States, the debate continues over exactly what the truth is behind the sightings of anomalous objects that are above the Earth. The U.S. Air Force has explained on many occasions that a lot of what is seen can be explained. However, with the obsession of extra-terrestrial mythology and reality, every bright light, shooting star, experimental plane, and weather anomaly can end up on the front pages of tabloid newspapers and on special fringe news programs labeled as bona fide extra-terrestrial craft with the acronym UFO attached to it.

The truth is that while much of what we think of UFO's can be attributed to cold war mythology, the reality has taken a turn for the complex and the use of experimental aircraft has now created a new discipline for the UFO researcher.

There is no denying that UFO's are out there; the truth, however, no longer is.

The old axiom of the "truth" being out there becomes trite and hollow as the identification process unveils both elaborate hoaxes and the frightening reality of remarkable aircraft designed by the military and, in some cases, by entities or intelligences far beyond our comprehension.

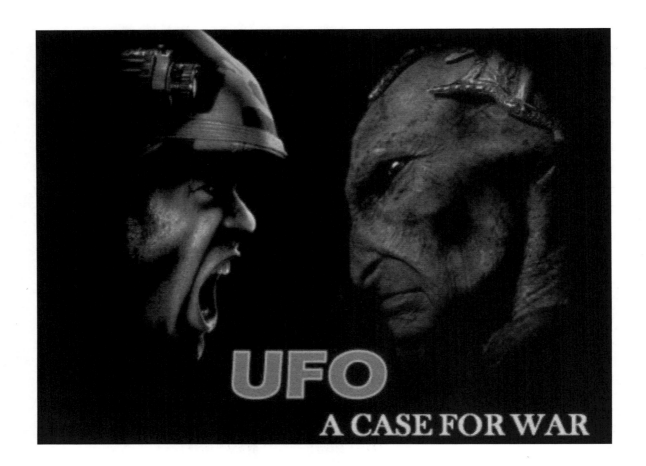

UFO: A CASE FOR WAR

There has always been a compelling argument that the military is fully aware that unidentified aerial phenomena exist and that the objects in question seem to have a connection to our oceans. Towards the end of 2011 and continuing into 2012, there were reports of anomalous sounds accompanied by equally strange smells of sulfur and ozone from Vancouver, British Columbia to Southern California. Much of what can be termed a putrid odor was believed to be coming from the oceans and according to some marine biologists was attributed to massive fish die offs.

In another report, strange sounds were heard in west Seattle. The sound was very whiny and mechanical. However the mainstream media had stated that there was evidence to suggest that the sounds could be attributed to fish mating in the Puget Sound.

Any reporter that saw this as a great mystery, and any news editor that demanded that a quick explanation be made to the public, has missed or purposefully overlooked the strange and mysterious incidents that have happened all year long.

It seemed that the mainstream media, fearful of what public opinion might say out of sheer panic, came up with some of the most ludicrous stories to explain anomalies.

The question is: if the mainstream media's explanation is to be believed, then why have the anomalous sounds and smells continued? There seems to be mounting evidence pointing to the possibility that these anomalies are either geomagnetic or extraterrestrial and have a far deeper cause. There is also the outrageous new claim that what we are witnessing is an extra-terrestrial or exo-biological event and that secretly, the scientists and military are busily trying to cover up the evidence of an alien intrusion.

In March of 2012 there were reports of strange rumbles up and down the west coast. Many of these reports were coming from Northern Washington and there were also reports of thunderous sounds and even mechanical hums near San Francisco, Northern Utah and Arizona.

The U.S. East Coast also was reporting a few UFO fireball sightings and at the time it seemed like a mini UFO flap was underway.

Later in the month there was a strange experiment being carried out on the east coast. NASA successfully launched 5 Missiles during their ATREX launch. The rockets carried trimethyl aluminum into the air to create a chemical trail that would cover the sky and allow science to study space winds.

Just three days prior to the ATREX launch there were reports of Earthquake swarms and UFO activity in Virginia and New York. Once again there were strange whining and rumbling noises that accompanied the events.

All of these cases seemed to have been happening along the Northeastern part of the United States and moved to the Northwest.

These anomalous activities continued on Vancouver Island. The RCMP reported that there were several reports of rumblings and bright sky lights being seen in Sooke and Oshawa.

There was also a photo submitted of what looked like a UFO "mother ship" in the sky Over Vancouver Island.

In April these sounds were heard again in Washington State. Whatever was going on it moved across a Northern parallel from East to west and then it moved south along the Pacific Coast. UFO reports continued on the southern beaches of the West Coast.

There was also a report filed that there was a secret aircraft that was being tested at the Whidbey Island Naval Airbase in Washington state.

It was later denied.

Soon after there were confirmed reports that the hypersonic X-514A was being tested in the pacific and that quite possibly most if not all of the UFO stories were put to rest as the aircraft moved at Mach 20 and broke up during its test flight.

For a time it was thought that whatever was happening there could be a logical and sane explanation. Apart from the fact that rumblings were heard along with mysterious and strange sightings it was all business as usual for the Military and other officials to say that there were no tests of any exotic craft of any kind.

But there were, and whether or not it could be attributed to hypersonic tests is still specious at best.

FIREBALL/UFO FLAP AUGUST/SEPTEMBER

In August of 2012 there were a very large number of fireball/UFO sightings all over the Northeast. There were other sightings in North Carolina, Tennessee and Kentucky. It seemed as if the UFO's were moving across the country and with a map you could see that there was most certainly movement. The UFO and Fireball sightings moved south and then re-appeared in the west:

In the early morning of September 13th, 2012 residents of California, Nevada, Utah, Colorado and New Mexico – were stunned by the appearance of a vivid luminescent trail high up in the atmosphere. Reports were pouring in that a UFO was seen approaching and then breaking up in the sky.

A sheriff's deputy in northern New Mexico said he witnessed "an explosion" and part of the object breaking apart from the main body. There was no report of the trail moving from the ground upwards. All that was reported was a strange fireball moving quickly across the sky coming from the west. It then exploded mid way and then surged upward separated into two fire balls and then fell.

The explanation of the light show was eventually given by the Military. The associated press reported that while many people were reporting what appeared to be a UFO war there was a simple explanation. The "explosion" was a normal separation of the first and second stages of the unarmed Juno ballistic missile that was fired at 6:30 a.m. MT from Fort Wingate near Gallup, N.M., said Drew Hamilton, a spokesman for the U.S. Army's White Sands Missile Range. The expended first stage landed in a designated area of U.S. Forest Service land.

The explanation seemed a bit odd because it was reported back in 1993 that Fort Wingate was shut down. According to Wikipedia it is now designated as a storage facility.

To add more weirdness to the story – the Associated press then went on to report that the missile "test" was also an interception exercise that morning.

"The Juno missile was then targeted by advanced versions of the Patriot missile fired from White Sands, about 350 miles (560 kilometers) away, as part of a test. Two of the missiles were fired and hit the incoming Juno missile, said Dan O'Boyle, a spokesman for the Redstone Arsenal in Alabama, which was in charge of the Patriots used in the test. The Patriot missiles kill incoming targets by direct strike and don't explode."

— The Associated Press

According the Shara Park of KSL news in Salt Lake City, the light show was seen in Utah, prompting residents to say that whatever was in the sky had to have been huge to have been seen so far north. Park also reported that the missile "returned to base." Since when do Missiles "return to base" especially when it appears that a rather large celestial unknown exploded and the military claims an unusual missile test over a now closed base.

Sure sounds like a contrived story to cover up a matter of national security. What if what the residents saw was indeed a UFO war? It sounds like it is a crazy notion however a new story has surfaced that indicates Military might is being used to engage UFO's off the coast of San Francisco.

Gordon Duff the senior editor of Veterans Today is reporting that Asian intelligence is reporting that a combined fleet operation between the US and China has been going on, a full combat operation against what is said to be a "highly unfriendly extra-terrestrial threat."

The verifications of the fleet operations have been many; there have been no confirmations from the US side though the ships have been seen by every vessel that makes it offshore. The true nature of both the threat and the extent of the multinational military force used is beyond any imaginable classification level.

The question is now what are we to believe?

The circumstantial evidence is indicating that there have been most definitely tests being done over populated areas during the year. There have been attempts at full UFO disclosure and predictive programming indicating that Military has been engaging UFOs and aliens throughout history.

Stories ranging from the 1952 Operation Mainbrace in the Baltic sea to the encounters at the east gate of Rendlesham Air force base in England where soldiers came upon a UFO in a forest in 1980.

The debate continues over exactly what the truth is behind the sightings of anomalous objects that are above the earth. The U.S. Air force has explained on many occasions that a lot of what is seen can be explained. However with the obsession of extraterrestrial mythology and reality, every bright light, shooting star, experimental plane, and weather anomaly can end up on the front pages of tabloid newspapers and on special fringe news programs labeled as bona fide extra terrestrial craft with the acronym UFO attached to it.

This time we have a rare occurrence where contemporary sightings have tall tales surrounding them, and we are seeing the manufacturing of evidence. Not from someone wanting to create a hoax, but from the military itself.

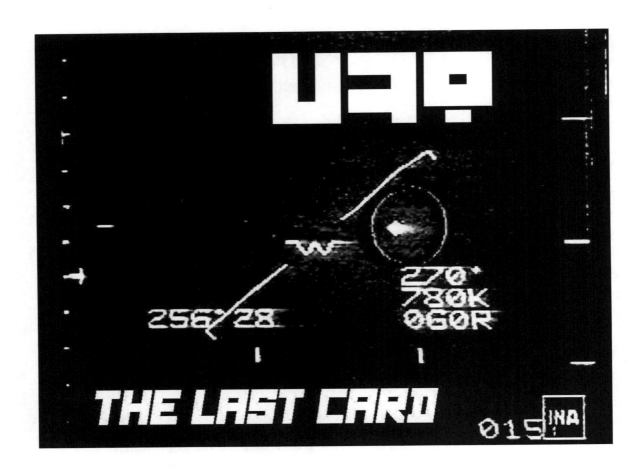

UFO: THE LAST CARD

NASA certainly has been bold lately, telling people not to panic about 2012, avoid any conversations about Planet X or space anomalies for fear it may upset the children. While NASA remains science's critical parent, they are also doing secret operations and not telling anyone about the fact that those space threats are very real. It is really hard for us to take the "Nothing to see here" attitude from NASA seriously, when they report doomsday scenarios with Global warming, and an asteroid with a propensity to wipe out earth sometime in the near future is passing over our heads on December 12th, 2012.

The near-Earth asteroid 4179 Toutatis which is about 3 miles wide, will zoom within 4.3 million miles of Earth during its closest approach early Wednesday morning. That's too far away to pose any impact threat on this pass but close enough to put on a pretty good show through top-notch telescopes.

What is also interesting is that in San Francisco there was a UFO sighting caught on many cell phones where many lights were seen in the sky creating geometric shapes. A flying triangular shaped object was seen floating in the Mission district of San Francisco once again without explanation. This happened on the weekend of December 7th, 2012. Science and skeptics are running out of logical answers as to what is seen in the sky. We no longer have a space shuttle flying over us and the ISS looks nothing like a flying triangle.

While we have been told that the shuttle program has been mothballed by NASA it is important to point out that the secret space program is alive and well. NASA has been in the news a lot lately leading us on into believing that there is nothing in space that we should be concerned with. They tell us that there is no life on mars and that there is no Planet X arriving to destroy the office Christmas party.

Meanwhile, the X-37b was launched on the back of an Atlas rocket. The rocket launched from launch complex 41. Launch commentary ended 17 minutes into the undisclosed mission. The X-37b had launched before and it continues to orbit the earth for some undisclosed reason.
The X-37B has been rumored to be part of a secret space patrol program that combs the area above the earth for any anomalies and reports back anything that can be a danger. It is also rumored that if a danger is detected then a message is sent back to earth to take action against any incoming threat.

There are many dangers looming in the heavens above us. There is always a chance that satellite with a lethal payload could fall and land in a populated area killing thousands of people, or some anomalous meteor or asteroid that could be heading for the planet.

There is of course the other theory and that is the idea that while we are going about our daily routines that there are intelligences out in space that are watching the planet and that there have been an increase of UFO reports in the year of 2012.

The Huffington Post reported a strange story about UFO's that has not been mentioned on the network newscasts and that is NASA has been secretly recording instances of UFO activity near Mars, the Moon and the International Space Station.

Last October more than 100 UFOs have been seen along the India-China border, and the sightings have officials puzzled. The Times of India reported this week that "yellowish spheres appear to lift off from the horizon on the Chinese side and slowly traverse the sky for three to five hours before disappearing."

The Times of India added that the UFO sightings have stumped numerous Indian military groups, including their air force, NTRO technical intelligence agency and the Indo-Tibetan Border Police. The Los Angeles Times reported that intelligence had ruled out the simple answer of the UFO's being Chinese drones or low-orbit satellites. Even though officials tried to calm the population with possible down to earth explanations the people were not convinced that the objects were from earth or even friendly.

Over the year of 2012 there have been new age gurus and other dime store prophets selling people on the idea that on the winter solstice date that we may see a confirmation of anomalous activity in space. This will include asteroids, meteors, comets and even reports of extra-terrestrial anomalies tied to some intelligent life outside of this world.

When working on stories dealing with UFO subject matter, the cases become routine and strange lights that are in the sky at night can always be explained away as some sort of star creating an optical illusion in the polluted air or extra bright landing lights by some plane.

However, 2012 has been one year that the explanations are not always satisfying and when 95% of most UFO sightings can be explained the 5% have been taking center stage and creating a lot of anxiety to observers on earth below.

Recently there have been a number of fireball sightings and UFO footage sighted all over the country and the mainstream can't keep up with the reports and most skeptics can't make up explanations that make any sense. Not that any of their explanations mean anything to those who don't have an agenda of debunking that which is unexplainable.

The truth is for every so called logical explanation from swamp gas to fish having sex there is simply a reason to look up and wonder why heaven is on fire with reports of strange lights and other anomalies that cannot be explained.

For example, a recent UFO and fireball flap in Texas yielded some strange magnetic activity that is compelling.

From McKinney to the White Rock Lake area and all the way south to Houston, a bright flash was reported in the sky on December 7th, 2012. NASA reports that the massive fireball created a huge flash and left a large trail in the sky. It also says that what was seen was a fragment from an asteroid that may have jettisoned and found its way to earth.

Typically stories like this are interesting to anyone witnessing the bright flash and quite possibly a loud boom — other than that we know that things coming from space enter our atmosphere and later explode and disintegrate. There was however another story that was in my opinion connected to the space anomalies over Texas. In fact, the event happened the day before the fireball or UFO arrived. Power poles in as many as five central Texas counties spontaneously exploded in flames and authorities were trying to find out why.

A Department of Public Safety communications officer said power poles in Hill, Falls, Bell, Williamson and McLennan counties mysteriously began bursting into flames at about 4 a.m. December 6th, 2012 He said the fires that had been reported were burning at the tops of the poles, some involving transformers. Various power company representatives had been dispatched to survey the damage and several fire departments were sent to douse the flames. This wasn't just a couple of poles arching and burning, the utility reported a total of 30 or more exploding. As many as 30 power poles were burning in one area of Hill County, just off Interstate 35 at mile marker 361. As many as 20 poles were reported burning in Bynum east of Hillsboro and others in the Aquilla area where some customers were without power.

There were poles on fire along Highway 6 near Falls County roads 112 and 113 that had forced closure of Highway 6 and had stopped trains along an adjacent railroad line for about an hour.

Some limited power outages were reported in the area around Perry, just north of Marlin. *"Power pole fires also were reported in at least two locations in Waco, just north of Troy, just south of the Falls County line on Interstate 35 in Bell County, near Lorena and west of Waco along U.S. Highway 84."* Areas of west Waco were without power after transformers failed near Hillcrest Hospital.

Authorities stated that they felt that low lying fog may have created a short circuit. However what they won't theorize is that a magnetic pulse could have caused the fires. Fireballs and UFO's have been known to be preceded by earthquakes or magnetic anomalies. They also have been known to happen simultaneously or even after the appearance.

On the evening of Saturday, March 12th, 2005 a UFO was seen in the sky by residents ranging from southern Oregon to Seattle, WA. The time of the sighting was a few minutes before 8 PM PST.

At approximately the same time, a 3.3 magnitude earthquake occurred nearby Olympia, WA. Just a few minutes later, a large power outage left thousands of Seattle residents without electricity for approximately an hour and a half. The UFO was later determined to be a fireball. There were also reports of transformer explosions and power poles burning after the incident. This begs the question was it really just a meteor or was it a UFO with a large magnetic field.

As meteors or even UFO's move through the electric field of the earth, it is not unreasonable to expect that energetic effects could disturb both tectonic plates and electrical power systems. This also happens when CME's come from the sun.

Last year the head of NASA, Charles Bolden issued a statement through the NASA Headquarters of Emergency Operations advising employees and their families to prepare for any and unforeseen emergency and/or disasters. This sent a wave of speculation that perhaps near earth objects or even a possible alien invasion could happen, or that the elite would pull their last card option in creating some reason to believe that an alien intervention was about to unfold.

NASA had been preparing for some on planet and off planet disaster with FEMA and their Operation Eagle Horizon. He opened his statements with "*I became aware of some things.*" what were those things and why is it such a mystery? There was also a continuity exercise that was termed a failure on November 9th 2011. There was a National Emergency Alert Drill with a Message from the President about a danger facing the earth from space. The danger apparently was taken directly from the script of "Deep Impact" where the President is alerted to a possible ELE event from space.

If there is any conspiracy theory or cover-up that can be considered it is that this is a multilevel attempt to construct Intel data about how we react to reports of strange anomalies in the sky. What the public thinks, how disinformation is distributed and how the internet reacts to government agencies and their reports of space threats and then withdrawing their warnings with no accountability.

There is compelling data and theory that the United States is currently launching its space platform programs and using UFO/ fireball data reports as intelligence data on public reaction.

NASA tracks a potential extraterrestrial threat and then they say that the threat doesn't exist or they say that whatever threat was out there it is gone now, or that it disappeared somewhere over the south pacific. The scenario could be carried out for 18 months or so – the drama increases with every threat where we think we are seeing a comet or asteroid and in reality we are looking at a extraterrestrial spacecraft. This scenario is similar to the story by Arthur C. Clarke called Rendezvous with Rama.

The "Rama" is the name of an alien star ship, initially mistaken for an asteroid and named after the king Rama who is considered to be the seventh Avatar of the Hindu god Vishnu. Clarke explains in the book that by the 22nd century, scientists have used the names of all the Greek and Roman mythological figures to name astronomical bodies, and have thus moved on to Hindu mythology. Rama is actually asteroid 31/439 and it has been detected by astronomers in the year 2130 while still outside the orbit of Jupiter. The object's speed (100 000 km/h) and the angle of its trajectory clearly indicate that this is not an object on a long orbit around our sun; it comes from interstellar space.

Astronomers' interest is piqued when they realize that this asteroid not only has an extremely rapid 4 minute rotation period but it is quite large in size for an asteroid. An unmanned space probe dubbed Sita is launched from the Mars moon Phobos, and photographs taken during its rapid flyby reveal that Rama is a mathematically perfect cylinder, 20 kilometres in diameter and 54 kilometres long, made of a completely featureless material. In other words, this is humankind's first encounter with an alien space ship.

The manned solar survey vessel Endeavour is sent to study Rama, as it is the only ship close enough to do so in the brief period of time Rama will spend in our solar system. Endeavour manages to rendezvous with Rama one month after the space ship first comes to Earth's attention, when the giant alien spacecraft already is within Venus' orbit. The 20+ crew, led by Commander Norton, enters Rama and explores the vast 16-km wide by 50-long cylindrical world of its interior, but the nature and purpose of the starship and its creators remains enigmatic throughout the book.

The only life forms on board Rama are the cybernetic "biots" who completely ignore the humans. All they want to do is refuel and be on their way. We as humans can't fathom why the biots have no interest in us.

The idea of crying wolf becomes an intelligence game with the public until they become desensitized to the conventional science fiction invasion and then the last card is pulled with the announcement happening at a moment when it is needed for world control.

Dr. Carol Rosin appeared on Ground Zero Radio in 2001. Rosin was the first woman corporate manager of Fairchild Industries and was spokesperson for Werner Von Braun in the last years of his life. She founded the Institute for Security and Cooperation in Outer Space in Washington DC and has testified before Congress on many occasions about space based weapons. What she had said to Ground Zero listeners concurs with what William Cooper had to say about faking a heavenly event.

Just before Von Braun died Rosin claims that Von Braun told her that the government will name several threats to the world that would create an urgency to organize a new government and build space weapons. Von Braun was well aware of certain "intelligence" because he was a part of the NAZI /U.S. protection plan called Operation paper Clip. Nazi scientists and intelligence officers were used to organize the space programs and the CIA. He claimed that the Russians would be the first enemy of concern, then Muslim Terrorists, with the final concern or what Von Braun called "The Last card" being an alien threat.

However, Von Braun stated that the Extra terrestrial threat would first be about near earth objects, like asteroids, and meteors. Then the threat would come from the Sun and finally we would be told to fear living Extra terrestrials that want to come down and kill us. Von Braun said that the Alien threat would be a lie. A hoax concocted to bring about a New World Order, a space based weapons platform and create a New World Religious movement.

The question is whether or not you believe the words of a known NAZI scientist or do you wonder if the anomalies we keep hearing about in space are part of an intel cover for a real alien landing or arrival. The idea for a stage alien threat has been around for a long time. However there is also the movement that is demanding disclosure of an alien or extraterrestrial presence among us.

Are we so certain that we are getting any objective information from authorities regarding what is going on in space? Do these cosmic events seem to indicate changes in space and perhaps a preparation for the arrival of an extraterrestrial civilization? Could we be witnessing the beginnings of the disclosure process where we are forced to look up and decide for ourselves if the objects near the sun are really planets, or asteroids, or even brown dwarf stars?

It has been suggested that there seems to be mounting tension is rising over the rumored plan of President Obama to announce the existence of intelligent life in outer space.

However, if secret space planes are being used to scour the skies, I don't believe that this will happen anytime soon.

UFO NORTHWEST: THE FIRST WAVE

We all know about UFO lore. However the history that gets buried beneath the Roswellian overkill is the first wave of UFO accounts. The Modern UFO era actually begins in the Northwest. From the Mountains of Washington on down to the farms of Oregon the alien infestation was already heating up long before the alleged alien crash at Roswell.

When thumbing through dime store book about UFO's the genesis always seems to be the crash of a flying disc in July of 1947somewhere near Roswell New Mexico. It seems that it all can be recited verbatim and most people will somehow let the story just fly over their heads never absorbing the details.

UFO cases become so academic at times that they can be a big yawn fest. Most UFO researchers have probably studied the Roswell crash over and over.

The on going investigation into the case can be tedious. Once you have nailed the history the case seems to trail off into all sorts of claims and hushed up witnesses. Most of them are dying off and so eventually there will be a tainted history that will eventually become "fact."

Perhaps the salvation of UFO history is to take a look at the first wave of the modern UFO stories. When we do so we trace them back to the American Northwest.

It seems that 1947 was the year the UFO pre history in the United States was centered in the Areas of Washington and Oregon.

On June 21, 1947 Harold A. Dahl was cruising in a boat that he operated with his partner Fred L. Crisman. During the afternoon Dahl and his 15-

year-old son were in the Puget Sound area near Maury Island Washington when they spotted six round objects that looked like flying doughnuts.

The doughnuts were circling one that looked like it was in trouble. It started sinking towards the boat. As the unknown aircraft was spinning it began to emit hot metal. The metal hit the boat and some of the slag burned his son. Other white hot metal ejecta landed and killed a dog that was on board. Dahl pulled towards Maury Island and began taking pictures of the event with a camera.

Dahl tried to radio for help, but it seemed that while the objects were overhead, the radio had too much interference and so the radio was of no use to the panicked harbor patrolman and his boy. Dahl took his son to Tacoma to treat his burns. He then told his partner Fred Crisman that the metal that damaged the boat was caused by some unidentified craft.

Later Dahl was visited by what could only be described as a stereotypical Man in Black. That man wore the black suit and also drove a brand-new 1947 Buick sedan. The MIB treated Dahl to Breakfast at a waterfront café and then after their meeting threatened Dahl. The MIB was also a witness to the UFO sighting and told Dahl that if he loved his family he would keep his mouth shut about the whole event.

Dahl Told Crisman again and Crisman demanded the photographic evidence. The film was useless. All of the exposures were fogged. Crisman then went to Maury Island and claimed that there was metal slag strewn all over the Island. While he was surveying the area a similar Doughnut shaped craft came roaring out of the clouds. Needless to say Crisman finally became a firm believer in Dahl's story.

On June 24, 1947 Roy Timm a 12 year old boy and his 18 year old brother were working on their Pendleton Oregon Ranch. His mother was on the porch observing he and his brother raising the telephone lines in front of the house in order to make room for hay trucks that pass through. Suddenly, three saucer shaped objects appeared in the sky above their ranch. The Objects whizzed by at a low altitude. Roy recalls that they were so low that he and his family could see windows along the side. They claim the saucers came form the southeast.

The next day the papers reported that a pilot saw nine objects in the sky above Mount Rainier. The Associated press released this article on June 25th, 1947.

PENDELTON, Ore., June 25 (AP) -- Nine bright saucer-like objects flying at "incredible speed" at 10,000 feet altitude were reported here today by Kenneth Arnold, a Boise, Idaho, pilot who said he could not hazard a guess as to what they were.

Arnold, a United States Forest Service employee engaged in searching for a missing plane, said he sighted the mysterious objects yesterday at 3 P.M. They were flying between Mount Rainier and Mount Adams, in Washington State, he said, and appeared to weave in and out of formation. Arnold said he clocked and estimated their speed at 1,200 miles an hour.

This was the story that gave birth to the term "flying saucer." A rash of UFO's seen in the Northwest in 1947 long before anything ended up in the Roswell Record. However contrary to popular belief the objects seen by Arnold were not saucers at all. In 1977 a memoir of the incident was given by Arnold for the First International UFO Congress. In a statement Arnold revealed that the flying saucer label came about because of a mistake. The reporter for the press, Bill Bequette asked him how the objects flew and Arnold answered that, "Well, they flew erratic, like a saucer if you skip it across the water." He used a metaphor to describe the objects and so the term was a misunderstanding. Arnold stated countless times that the objects "were not circular."

A few quotes from Arnold show that there was a great deal of UFO activity in the skies of the Northwest on that day in 1947:

"There was a DC-4 to the left and to the rear of me approximately fifteen miles distance, and I should judge, at 14,000 foot elevation. The sky and air was clear as crystal. I hadn't flown more than two or three minutes on my course when a bright flash reflected on my airplane. It startled me as I thought I was too close to some other aircraft.

I looked every place in the sky and couldn't find where the reflection had come from until I looked to the left and the north of Mt. Rainier where I observed a chain of nine peculiar looking aircraft flying from north to south at approximately 9,500 foot elevation and going, seemingly, in a definite direction of about 170 degrees.

They were approaching Mt. Rainier very rapidly, and I merely assumed they were jet planes. Anyhow, I discovered that this was where the reflection had come from, as two or three of them every few seconds would dip or change their course slightly, just enough for the sun to strike them at an angle that reflected brightly on my plane. These objects being quite far away, I was unable for a few seconds to make out their shape or their formation.

Very shortly they approached Mt. Rainier, and I observed their outline against the snow quite plainly. I thought it was very peculiar that I couldn't find their tails but assumed they were some type of jet plane. I was determined to clock their speed, as I had two definite points I could clock them by; the air was so clear that it was very easy to see objects and determine their approximate shape and size at almost fifty miles that day."-Kenneth Arnold

A few weeks later a crash of a "flying disc" was later reported in New Mexico near Roswell. However after later research this so called saucer was definitely not a saucer but a craft that looked more like a flying chevron aircraft. The focus on the Roswell case and the strange craft that crashed there was an eager interest into the origins of where these craft had come from. Were they from another world? Or were they secret experimental craft that would eventually be revealed at a later date, or during a later military conflict?

While the saucer has shown up in many photos turned over by anxious witnesses it is interesting to note that saucer hysteria had gripped Hollywood after the initial reports out of the Northwest.

Saucer shapes turned up in movies like "The day the earth stood Still" and "Earth vs. the flying saucers."

Then came a controversial photo again out of the Northwest.

The Mcminnville Oregon/ Trent photos have always been a contentious case and for decades many debunkers have claimed that the photos are hoaxes. However there has been no concrete proof to show that Paul and Evelyn Trent, the farmers who snapped the photos in May of 1950 were perpetrating a hoax.

Paul and Evelyn Trent snapped these photos on their farm just before sunset on May 11th, 1950. The negatives of the pictures were situated in the middle of the film roll. Upon inspection there were no practice photos indicating that the Trents had developed a hoax. The photos sat in the camera an entire month before they were developed at a drugstore. The photos were featured in Life Magazine in June of 1950.

The photos sat in the Trent home before they garnered any notoriety. It is told in the annals of UFO lore that the Trents had waited until the roll of film was finished before they even said anything.

Funny how they waited.

Maybe they were not UFO nuts and actually waited until they were sure of what they caught on film. The other interesting thing to note is that the photos were in the middle of the roll of film. There were no practice shots of the UFO and no other evidence to show that they were trying to create a hoax. Just two photo negatives showing an anomalous object buried amongst the mundane pictures of family and friends.

The photos turned out to be some of the first that ended up in a newspaper. If the people wanted to see a disc this was the best one, it was the closest one anyone ever captured.

On June 8, 1950 the McMinnville, Oregon Telephone Register displayed on its front pages two photographs of what is now known as the McMinnville Oregon UFO.

"At long Last photos of an authentic flying Saucer?" That was the headline on the front page of the McMinnville Telephone Register in June of 1950. The photos in the story were later declared two of the clearest UFO photographs on record.

On June 10th, 1950 the story broke every where else and a saucer hungry public saw the pictures. Stories ran in all the papers. It was reported that Evelyn Trent was outside working on the family farm near Dayton Oregon. Dayton is about 11 miles south of McMinnville Oregon (USA). Evelyn then claims she looked up and noticed a strange metallic object in the sky. She yelled for her husband to grab a camera. He ran outside and snapped the two famous photos. The photos eventually landed in a Life magazine feature on June 26th, 1950.

There have been many debunkers who have claimed that the stories had changed at every report. However as I pointed out earlier Kenneth Arnold never said that he saw a flying saucer. The media said so and it stuck. The stories given by the Trents could have changed as well and the question still stands as to why it took them a moth to get the photos developed. Obviously they didn't see it as news worthy or of urgency.

In fact the photos themselves would not have even made it into the McMinnville Telephone register if it weren't for the eye of a reporter who saw them hanging in a bank window.

Later people would actually show up on the farm to look around. Some would even throw hubcaps in the air to see if they could get the same effect. It obviously didn't work.

The Trents were just simple farmers. They obviously weren't flying saucer seekers, or UFO nuts out to make a fast buck. Paul Trent even said at one time that he believed that the picture that he captured was that of a secret Military aircraft.

There was no talk of alien beings or men from Mars at the time. You can leave all of that cosmic talk to the journalists of the day. The Trents may have received some fame from the photos. But it seems that they never really made much money. You can also sit and ponder why these photographs and the other stories out of the Northwest have been downplayed in UFO lore for some reason.

They were actually the first UFO events that pre dated UFO hysteria brought on by the events at Roswell.

There is always a prevailing attitude amongst smug debunkers that flying saucer photographs were snapped with the same zeal back in the early days of the "flaps" as they may be today. In the Trent case it seems that these attitudes do not wash. When was the last time a physicist has written books about the Northwest UFO cases? When have you seen documentaries that have set the record straight about the unidentified aircraft spotted in the Northwest in the 1940's and 1950's? They get a quick mention in most presentations and the details of the mistakes that were made in reporting these cases get overlooked.

If the cases were reopened would we have a different attitude about unidentified flying objects? Would it have a more mundane explanation? Would it have changed history? Would there have been a better attitude about these aircraft and the investigation?

I believe that the answer is yes.

Both Paul and Evelyn Trent died in the late 1990s. The house where the photographs were taken has long since been torn down.

UFO: SPHERE OF INFLUENCE

The sun has become increasingly active lately and, with the increase of magnetic effects on the earth, Ufologists have also become "increasingly active." In fact, Ufologists all over the world are claiming that the year 2012 is living up to its reputation as being a year for supernatural events and UFO activity.

When we first witnessed increased solar activity in January there were reports of planet sized UFO's is seen near the sun. One object was a spheroid, while another looked perfectly square and yet another was a pyramid shaped object that still have amateur astronomers scratching their heads and NASA struggling to find a plausible denial that they can report to the consensus reality While many faithful Planet X gazers are thinking that a huge spheroid object is coming our way and that it will bring with it cataclysm we must understand that more and more reports in the nightly news are showing that most of the UFO's recently reported have been round much like a small planet or probe.

A recent capture of video from the solar observatory shows that large dark spheres of unknown origin have parked above the sun. They are shown extracting magnetic energy from the sun's surface. The Filament of energy appears to be a giant vortex that has attached to the sphere like a gigantic umbilical cord. The sphere then moves away and an energy burst causes the vortex to break down.

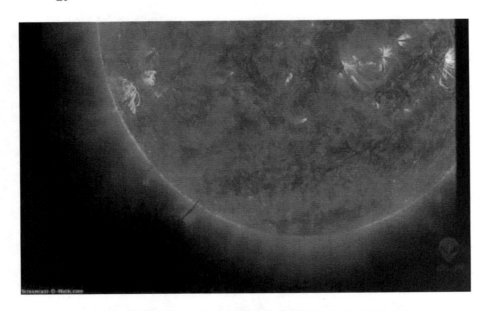

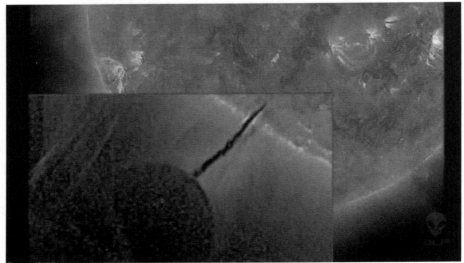

Some of the more famous UFO's in history have been described as large orbs and not necessarily having characteristics of Flying Triangles or Discs.

On July 11th 1991 during an eclipse of the sun Mexican nationals looked up into the sky and with Video cameras in hand managed to get on tape the appearance of several Orbs hovering in the skies and then moving erratically. Some were disc shaped and others looked like small shimmering Christmas Tree ornaments flying in formation.

In March of 1997 a chain of events took place that eventually led to the deaths of 39 people Near San Diego California.

Not only was the world gazing into the skies to see the Comet Hale Bopp but others were seeing things that had them wondering if an invasion had begun.

Glowing orbs or spheres made their presence known and many people were frightened and demanded answers. March 13th 1997, will be a day that will be remembered as the day of the most remarkable American UFO Sighting ever recorded.

It will be remembered as the Phoenix Lights incident where Glowing orbs made a huge triangular formation over a 300-mile corridor from the Nevada line through Prescott Valley and Phoenix to the northern edge of Tucson. Later in the night, a series of bright spheres appeared on the city's southern horizon. It was later reported that the orbs and the appearance of a a mile long triangular aircraft hovering in the night sky were two separate events.

The event was at first ridiculed by local officials as a trick of light and possible flares from nearby Luke air force base. However it was later revealed by then Governor Fife Symington and Senator John McCain that the UFO threat over Phoenix was very real and to this day both the wedge "Triangular Craft" and the sightings of orbs remain a mystery.

Then came the stories from amateur astronomers that a glowing orb was caught in the gravitational pull of Comet Hale Bopp. This so impressed Marshall Applewhite, the leader of the Heaven's gate Cult that he was willing to believe that this was a sign that the God's were returning. Especially those who dwelled in the Evolutionary Level Above Human.

Applewhite convinced 38 of his followers to commit suicide for a chance to ride on what has been called "the companion" an alleged beam ship that was in the tail of the comet. After the bodies of the dead cult members were taken from scene, the people who were responsible for reporting that a "companion" was following Hale Bopp were silenced. Others were chastised for reporting dangerous information. After the initial shock had wound down it was later reported that Zdenek Sekanina of NASA's Jet Propulsion Laboratory confirmed that a natural satellite about 33 kilometers wide was orbiting about 200 kilometers from Hale-Bopp's nucleus. The Orb in the tail of the Comet was very real and not a hoax.

The spheroid UFO phenomena are becoming more common now than ever. While many unknown craft can be misidentified the orbs and sphere's in the night time or day time sky seem to be the most common in 2012. Many of these spheres are being reported as being reflective of surrounding lights, floating mysteriously and silently as if observing the ground below. Then they quickly disappear like bubbles blown from a wand and then bursting in mid air.

While many will scoff and say that the spheres are flares or balloons, it has to be revealed that many f these spheres have fallen to earth and have been recovered in remote areas.

An unidentified metal sphere plunged from the sky on unsuspecting villagers in northern Brazil on February 23rd, 2012. There was a thunderous explosion as the sphere entered the atmosphere and crashed in a remote area. According to eyewitnesses, the UFO weighs about 50 kilograms and measures roughly one meter in diameter. The sphere fell on the village of Riacho dos Poços in Brazilian Maranhão state. No casualties were reported apart from a cashew tree that was destroyed by the object as it plunged to the ground. Video was shot of the sphere and it is still unknown where it came from.

On March 9th, 2012 just 15 days before the anniversary of the Phoenix lights there was an unbelievable explosion of light that was caught on camera during the morning traffic report on KSAZ TV in Phoenix. As KSAZ's Andrea Robinson delivered a traffic update, a mysterious sphere or orb of bright light appeared in the live shot over the tree line near a Phoenix highway.

KSAZ checked with local utilities companies to see if perhaps a transformer had blown, but there were no reports of such an explosion. They also added that there was no sign of any extraterrestrial vehicles however the phenomena may had been the result of the magnetic fluctuations during Solar flare activity that was happening at the time. Around the same time I was notified of a strange rumbling noise that was being felt and heard in Hillsboro Oregon, Rachel had notified me via Facebook that the rumbling sound at first sounded like thunder and then it sounded mechanical and coming from the sky. She also reported that near the full moon there were what appeared to be clouds in the sky similar to a "funnel" or "vortex" formation. Inside the Vortex was a bright sphere.

I was unable to get the sound until I received an e-mail from someone who lived near Cornelius Oregon that said that he believed the sound was coming from Forest Grove. The sound was recorded on a cell phone and really sounded like thunder. I listened carefully to the recording and began to notice a tone or whine in the rumble. It sounded like a jet engine or perhaps something more? I couldn't tell.

I decided to feature the sound on my radio show to see if anyone had heard the same sound. A few callers had said that they had heard the sound. I decided to send a message back in the form of a low frequency hum made by the Aboriginal instrument known as the didgeridoo. I had actually done an experiment similar in Utah and it was later reported on Fox 13 news by Dave Candland that there were UFO's sighted over the Ogden Utah area the night I broadcast the tones.

I asked my audience to step outside to see if there was any UFO activity. The sky was overcast and the only real reports of anomalous activity was more rumbles in Washington county and a few flashes of light being seen in the sky.

I left the station to catch my bus home and I phoned Olav Phillips my producer in Northern California to report on the show. As I was waiting for the bus and chatting with Olav there was a person at the bus stop that said "What the hell is that?" I looked up and just barely clearing the buildings at about 400 feet was a round spherical object.

It did not make a sound and my first thought was that it was a Mylar balloon reflecting the amber lighting of the street below. It actually reminded me of the bubble that came floating down in the Wizard of Oz, when Dorothy meets the good witch.

I then spoke up and said "Wow what is that up there?"

Olav said literally "Hang up the phone and take a picture dumb ass!" I obliged and nervously pushed the buttons on my phone to get a picture. I pointed upwards and clicked the phone. Just as I heard the phone click I saw that the spherical object had flashed a bright green and then disappeared. I thought that I had just missed the opportunity to get the UFO on camera. After I looked at the camera I realized that I caught the sphere as it was disappearing leaving what looked like a green torus shape in the sky.

The object made no sound; it hovered in the sky near the buildings then hovered over 6th avenue. It had an amber glow and was actually reflecting the lights below. As I drew my camera it darted west and reflected or made a green glow – it then disappeared. The sphere could not have been more than 10-12 feet in diameter. It looked like a bubble or a jelly fish.

It was not an orb, it seemed to have a membrane surrounding it where it came out from the top like a fountain and then arching around like a deformed sphere or heart shape.

I have seen UFO's, orbs and the like, however this looked peculiar. I first thought of something logical when I saw it, however when it hovered I knew it wasn't at all normal and the way it popped out of site with a green light made it even more interesting.

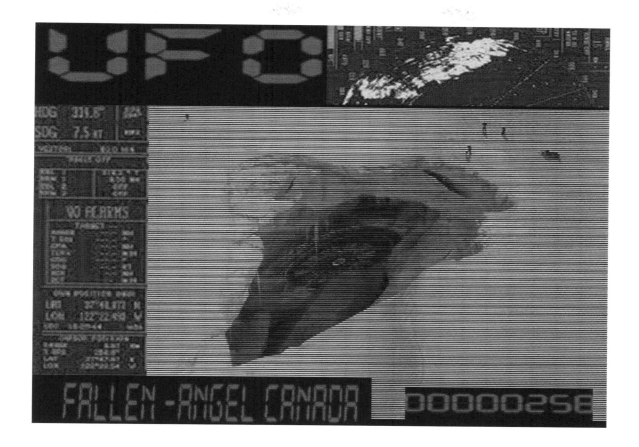

UFO: FALLEN ANGEL CANADA

This weekend I was notified that a recent UFO sighting, involving a dramatic crash into Lake Winnipeg in Canada has now gotten the attention of amateur UFO researchers and those who wish to debunk the crash as some sort of experiment gone wrong.

The UFO report was first filed on Facebook by a man named Brent Mancheese, who snapped a few photos in the area of the crash and posted them on his news feed.

Lake Winnipeg prior to crash

Immediately his Facebook page had been taken down. The UFO crash, which garnered attention for the dramatic nature of the military UFO cover-up involved, occurred near Jackhead, Manitoba. With this event standing as one of the most dramatic UFO incidents of the past several months

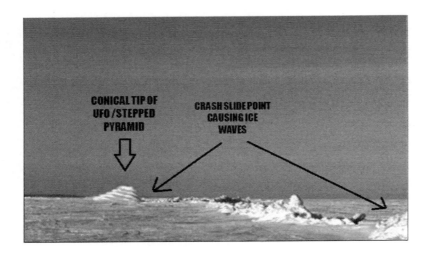

Crash site in Jackhead

Military trucks seen in Jackhead

Another dramatic UFO encounter happened in Peru during a television interview.

A television production crew in Lima, Peru, videotaped a purple-colored disc-shaped UFO hovering in the distant sky near a construction site. So far, there's no official explanation for the object.

According to *Peru This Week*, the TV show "Alto al Crimen" was shooting an episode in the upscale Miraflores district of Lima on February 10. The show's host, Lima Congressman Renzo Reggiardo, halted an interview to allow his camera operator to focus on the strange-looking purple object in the sky.

UFO seen live on TV show "Alto al Crimen."

The object was a classic disc shaped object that was just hovering over a construction site giving off a strange purple and blue color.

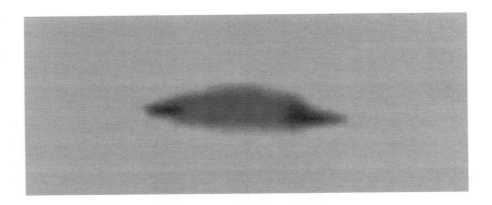

Purple UFO seen in Peru

Meanwhile the Canadian UFO crash kept gaining ground as residents in the area of Jackhead told that there was a shelter in place in effect and that all cell phone and computer communications would be halted until the craft was safely pulled out of the ice and the danger was clear. Literally, the Canadian military had blocked communications about the incident, which brings up a lot of questions that I am sure the military does not want to answer.

UFOs of course are a hard sell in a world where skepticism has taken hold all because of internet opportunists that love a good UFO story that they can hoax or use to fool the public.

It seems there was indeed something in the ice of military interest on Feb. 18. Pictures of military vehicles near Jackhead were popping up all over the internet, generating from twitter accounts in Winnipeg.

People described the vehicle as looking like a stepped up pyramid about 200 yards long and triangular shaped. One resident commented that whatever the craft was, it was huge and had a long set of lights and literally broke in two. Pieces of it were seen heading straight up and then dropping suddenly into the lake causing a huge wave that pushed the ice up into huge piles.

CBC news was alerted to all of the talk of UFOs and decided to investigate. What they reported was that it was not a UFO at all, according to Lt.-Col. Paul Davies, commanding officer 38 Territorial Battalion Group. He claimed that the battalion is involved with an Arctic

Response Company Group training exercise on Lake Winnipeg called Arctic Bison 2015

Members of the Arctic Response Company Group drive across frozen Lake Winnipeg during Exercise Arctic Bison 2015.

About 150 military personnel are taking part in Exercise Arctic Bison 2015, which includes the 38 Canadian Brigade Group, the 2nd Battalion of the Princess Patricia's Canadian Light Infantry, the 4th Canadian Ranger Patrol Group, and 440 Squadron of the Royal Canadian Air Force.

Davies said soldiers are training to deal with a plane crash and provide ground search and rescue support in the Arctic.

The bright light that people saw, he explained, came from an airplane that takes off very quickly and then crashes.

Residents were not aware of this exercise and during the UFO incident a very harsh cold front has blown through making it dangerous to be outside. It is also peculiar that a shelter in place command has been issue for the area. Nobody is allowed to leave or enter the reservation at this time and that the military has been going door to door talking with residents. They are telling the residents that they are conducting emergency training exercises.

If it routine training why all of the drama, why is there a shelter in place command being issued by the military and with the extreme cold front in Manitoba over the last two days why would these so called exercises continue in extremely dangerous conditions. In a deadly freeze, it is dangerous to spend time outdoors for any period.

The military has moved in all their equipment effectively blocking any view of what may have crashed into the water or what they are doing there.

We contacted Peter Davenport from the National UFO Reporting Center. He tells us that he had contacted Dr. Chris Ruthowski from the Canadian

UFO report in Manitoba and the strike team from MUFON and they claim there is nothing to the story.

What we lack are credible witnesses in this story. The few that have talked are now being told not to. The evidence was not first presented to a credible news agency. Even if a UFO crashed in the waters of Jackhead, there would be a hardly anyone that could accurately get near it. All we have are a few curious pictures and some commentary that something evidently crashed there.

Again it is a matter of who do you trust, the military's explanation or what people saw?

The UFO community is frequently inundated with promises of easy answers. Insiders emerge with convenient explanations about what is being seen, and with the latest Blue Book revelations there is more caution now about what is reported and what is left to be ignored. It is always interesting to see what UFO stories eventually become easily explained away by the military and which ones aren't explained and how long it will take for the story to get lost somewhere in the memory hole.

Many people in the field of research sincerely wants to believe that UFOs piloted by aliens is a common thing, but the truth is there are many theories that presume that perhaps the alien UFOs are rare and that what we are experiencing is the result of alien probes or unmanned or Artificial intelligence now pilots these aircraft.

In October of 2012, more than 100 UFOs were seen along the India-China border, and the sightings had officials puzzled. *The Times of India* reported that "yellowish spheres appeared to have lifted off from the horizon on the Chinese side and slowly traversed the sky for three to five hours before disappearing."

The Times of India added that the UFO sightings stumped numerous Indian military groups, including their air force, NTRO technical intelligence agency and the Indo-Tibetan Border Police. *The Los Angeles Times* reported that intelligence had ruled out the simple answer of the UFOs being Chinese drones or low-orbit satellites. Even though officials tried to calm the population with possible down to earth explanations the people were not convinced that the objects were from earth or even friendly.

In fact a photographer who had witnessed this phenomenon began shooting pictures. What he witnessed was something that even baffled him. What he saw were orbs and spheres but what he also witnessed was what appeared to be machines with what appeared to be mechanical arms picking up spoil samples.

It was suggested that this was an extraterrestrial probe looking for earth soil. The theory lasted a long time and got the attention and the imagination of the people in China and India. In 2014, however, the media suggested that the UFOs in question were Chinese balloons gathering information and positions of troops along Chinese border. China is on altogether different level as compared to Indians in terms of technological advancement in military operations. The highly advanced robots that were used at the border have not been explained satisfactorily.

It is stating the obvious to say that everybody who does UFO research has at one time or another wished for the one great event — the ultimate smoking gun — that would decisively reveal the truth. Unfortunately, there is no shortcut. UFO research is just plain hard work.

In Ufology, a close encounter or CE is an event in which a person witnesses an unidentified flying object. This terminology and the system of classification behind it was started by astronomer and UFO researcher J. Allen Hynek, and was first suggested in his 1972 book *The UFO Experience: A Scientific Inquiry*. He introduced the first three kinds of encounters; more sub-types of close encounters were later added by others, but these additional categories are not universally accepted by UFO researchers.

Most are familiar with the term "Close Encounters of the Third Kind" because of the Steven Spielberg film which introduced the pop culture to UFO encounters. As UFO encounters have became more sophisticated there have been more terminologies associated with such encounters.

These numeric terminologies were added after Hynek's scientific studies.

CE-4: A UFO event in which a human is abducted by a UFO or its occupants. This type was not included in Hynek's original close encounters scale

Hynek's erstwhile associate Jacques Vallee argued in the *Journal of Scientific Exploration* that a CE4 should be described as "cases when witnesses experienced a transformation of their sense of reality," so as to also include non-abduction cases where absurd, hallucinatory or dreamlike events are associated with UFO encounters.

CE-5: A UFO event that involves direct communication between aliens and humans. This type of close encounter was named by Steven M. Greer's CSETI group. Those of this type are described as bilateral contact experiences through conscious, voluntary and proactive human-initiated cooperative communication with extraterrestrial intelligence.

CE-6: Death of a human or animal associated with a UFO sighting. Close Encounters of the Seventh Kind –The creation of a human/alien hybrid, either by sexual reproduction or by artificial scientific methods.

There are also military terms for UFOs. There are "Bogeys," "Santa Claus," and, if they crash, they are known as "Fallen Angels." The term also refers to a military craft that has crashed with a pilot inside.

The investigation of UFO sightings involves many hours spent interviewing witnesses, surveying sighting locations, collecting photos and evidence, digging through archives, and even going to the site itself to investigate.

I would say for the sake of argument that since the temperatures at Jackhead and Lake Winnipeg are so frigid and dangerous, all reports from outside sources should be considered spurious. The only people that know what has happened to them are the residents of the area and of course the military knows as well.

The sad thing is we often find out about sightings long after they happen — when the trail has become stone cold. Other times the trail of evidence leads to a dead end: Witnesses don't agree, somebody lies, evidence is lost or compromised, or an event turns out to be a hoax. Yet still we persevere. Eventually we see the fuzzy beginnings of a picture of the UFO phenomenon – but still we find no smoking gun. There are no easy answers.

UFO: WAKE UP TO THE NEW COVER UP

The phenomenon of UFOs is always a fascinating topic and a problematic one as well. While reporting UFO sightings for example, when can get caught up in location, and frequency. It is important for the investigator to understand the geographic area of a sighting and to know a little bit about airline approaches and other such locales that may contribute to mistaken sightings and oddities.

UFO reports that are just reports are good for research and comparison; however the best evidence is what can be gathered with pictures and video recording. Even with recordings of various lights in the sky at night and anomalous aircraft in the day, there will always be an armchair analyst that is willing to make up supposed "proof" of faking or hoaxing in order to thwart investigations into the UFO sighting or possible flap.

Like many 'fringe' subjects, there are scattered bits of solid information floating in a frothing sea of mythology, speculation, and disinformation. If the UFO happens to be a falsehood, more than likely an investigator will be ridiculed and accused of perpetrating the hoax.

Internet video captures a lot of attention on YouTube, and so with sophisticated software, would be special effects artists have created some remarkable footage. This footage appears to be so real even experts can be fooled.

The Internet video that is created by skilled hoaxers is now part of the new cover up of UFO activity and so those who participate in sophisticated hoaxes are part of the plan to keep UFO sightings secret and are used as disinformation to discourage anyone from even considering that UFO sightings are happening. Investigators call these attempts at hoaxing "noise."

The sheer volume of noise and confusion in the field of UFOlogy is staggering. There are those attempting to suppress and obfuscate the truth, and even more simply attempting to profit from the tremendous interest by manufacturing hoaxes.

This distracts from unusual or potentially dangerous sightings that are and in some cases give many people the reason to disbelieve or reject that UFO's, mainly aircraft unidentified do not exist. A belief that all unidentified objects are piloted by aliens does not help the cause of critical investigation either.

The potential danger of UFO's can be a threat to national security. Unidentified flying craft can very well be missiles, stealth aircraft, or even unknown technology from an enemy of the United States. There are also many people who mistakenly write off UFO sightings as drones, however drones are rare and in some states are considered illegal to fly anywhere without the right clearances or permits. There is currently no federal regulation of unmanned aircraft, but Congress passed a law two years ago ordering the FAA to issue national rules legalizing drones for commercial purposes by September 2015. There are still arguments over recreational drones and whether or not they should be illegal – or considered model aircraft.

In 2011, the FAA penalized drone videographer Raphael Pirker $10,000 for using a drone. Pirker challenged the fine, and a federal administrative-law judge overturned the penalty, saying there was no law banning the commercial use of small drones.

This month The FAA released its interpretation of rules for model aircraft after recent incidents involving reckless use of drones. The FAA states that hobby or recreational flying doesn't require FAA approval, but recommends following their safety guidelines, which encourage contacting the airport operator when flying within 5 miles of an airport, not flying near manned aircraft or beyond the operator's line of sight. It also specifies model aircraft as weighing fewer than 55 lbs.

Model aircraft operators were encouraged to voluntarily comply with the standards, which include not flying higher than 400 feet and notifying the airport operator when operating within 3 miles of an airport.

Complacency is the greatest weakness in the security of the USA. A small drone can be used by any terrorist to carry an explosive device to any target inside the USA. If it was sighted as a UFO and not reported, we could easily see the terrorists utilize the cover of a UFO sighting to carry out a terrorist attack.

The national security apparatus is becoming so proficient in protecting us from ourselves that they seem to be ignoring the idea that we may have real enemies waiting at our borders and, in some cases, testing their weapons in plain sight.

The security apparatus is so good at selecting suspects from their own style of homegrown paranoia that they pour a great deal of money into projects that violate civil rights while above us the skies are wide open for unforeseen events. Budgets that would protect us – from the various fireballs, UFO's and weapons tests that people are now seeing, reporting, and being told to shut up about – have been cut.

The debate continues over exactly what the truth is behind the sightings of anomalous objects that are above the Earth. The U.S. Air Force has explained on many occasions that a lot of what is seen can be explained.

However, with the obsession of extra-terrestrial mythology and reality, every bright light, shooting star, experimental plane, and weather anomaly can end up on the front pages of tabloid newspapers and on special fringe news programs labeled as bona fide extra-terrestrial craft with the acronym UFO attached to it.

A mysterious object lit up the dark sky in the southeast about an hour after midnight. The sighting was captured in Georgia, South Carolina, and Alabama.

It was described as a bright ball of light moving fast across the sky. It made a trail and was also seen with other lights accompanying it. The same can be said of a fireball or UFO that was spotted over Hillsboro, Oregon. Two lights were seen chasing each other. One flashed an eerie green and the other flashed a red and gold light. They eventually disappeared.

FLASHING ANOMALOUS LIGHTS SEEN OVER HILLSBORO OREGON 6/28/15

Meanwhile a sighting was also reported in Welches, Oregon near Mt. Hood. Dan Coe who works at a hotel in the area said that there was a thunderstorm in the area and as he was looking at the lightning he notice a clearing in the night sky. In that clearing he saw a UFO and happened to snap a picture of it before it disappeared.

NASA informed everyone that the strange lights people were seeing everywhere was space junk coming down into the atmosphere. NASA has been accused of hiding proof of extraterrestrial life after it cut short a live stream from the International Space Station which, appeared to, show three UFO's fleeing the Earth. The footage was reportedly captured from NASA's ISS live cam feed, and shows three objects rising out of Earth's atmosphere.

UFO appears at the ISS Just before the Live Feed is Cut 6/8/2014.

NASA was reportedly forced to end a live stream from the International Space Station as three UFOs blasted into space.

But this is not the first time conspiracy theorists claim NASA has inadvertently captured extra terrestrial activity.

Live streams from the International Space Station have triggered hundreds of viral videos showing UFO's approaching or flying past the station.

One of the more popular videos shows the feed at night, suddenly an arrowhead shaped UFO appears at the ISS Just before the Live Feed is cut 6/8/2014.

Meanwhile there has been debate as to whether or not NASA is waiting to divulge information about extra terrestrial anomalies. There has been a lot of talk online about the sighting of huge pyramid and bright lights on the Dwarf planet CERES and a possible pyramid that has been revealed to be on Mars by the mars Rover.

Earlier this year there was speculation that the Rosetta project's Philae probe that landed on comet 67P had made communication with aliens and then it inexplicably shut down.

Philae, the first spacecraft to land on a comet, phoned home again on June 14th, 2015 and made contact with the European Space Agency ending its seven month silence.

The next probe that NASA will attempt to launch is the Origins Spectral Interpretation Resource Identification Security Regolith Explorer. Narrowed down to a mere acronym the aircraft will be called OSIRIS REX.

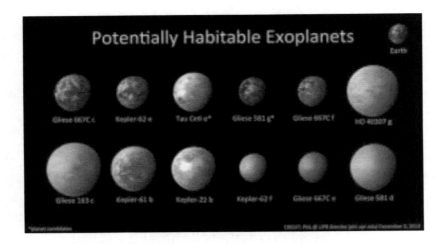

Its destination is the asteroid Bennu. Born in a violent collision millions of years ago, Bennu can tell us more about the story of the solar system, perhaps even the story of our origin.

Bennu is the Egyptian deity associated with the Phoenix. The Bennu was a self-created being said to have played a role in the creation of the world. It was said to be the Ba (that is, the spirit) of Ra and enabled the creative actions of the sun god Atum. It was said to have flown over the Egyptian waters of "Nu" that existed before creation, landing on a rock and issuing a call that determined the nature of creation. It was also a symbol of rebirth and was therefore associated with Osiris the father and Isis the mother goddess. The Bennu was a heron bird that would die and then would be reborn on the "Benben stone" as the first rays of the new dawn would arrive.

Earlier this month, NASA and university scientists hosted a panel in Washington D.C. to discuss the latest advancements in the search for life, with the focus on habitable planets. Another similar discussion – focused on water in the universe – was held on April 7, 2015, also in Washington D.C. At the April discussion, NASA chief scientist Ellen Stofan made a bold statement when she predicted that we would find "strong indications" of microbial life within a decade and "definite evidence" of it within 20 to 30 years.

At the same time, NASA also released an info graphic outlining evidence for or indications of water on a number of worlds in our solar system. Those worlds with possible water include the dwarf planet Ceres, now being orbited by the Dawn spacecraft, a world with two mysterious bright spots that might be icy plumes. And NASA included Jupiter's moon Europa on its new info graphic. This month, NASA announced that it was moving forward with plans to send a spacecraft to study Europa, which was found recently to have salt water in the dark fractures on its surface. That salt water is presumably from the liquid ocean thought to lie below Europa's frozen crust.

NASA has now outlined its plan to search for alien life and said it would launch the Transiting Exoplanet Surveying Satellite in 2017.
With all of this interest in extra-terrestrials and possible life and discovery, the question is why NASA insists on shutting down its live feed whenever something unidentified decides to bump up next to the ISS or decides to take off from planet earth.

NASA is good at taking down live feeds, but is becoming worse at covering up the fact that they know something is in space. Either we see it with our telescopes or we can detect it with instruments that can see what we don't see.

Einstein, along with many, many wise teachers, have all said that the invisible is more important and meaningful than the visible. As a species we are just now evolving into that realization. Maybe 5% of Earth's population actually understands something of this concept. Most of the rest of us still believe in only what our five senses can convey despite the fact that when we touch, or pick up an object we are holding mostly empty space.

Evolved aliens would likely have grown beyond our archaic and erroneous idea that the material world is all that really matters. Evolved aliens, therefore, would have learned to partner the visible and the invisible in their quantum "technology."

That being the case, we might well be having visitations on any number of levels and be completely unaware of them.

In the last century anthropologists found a number of "primitive" tribes hidden in the jungles and were delighted to study them, but had no wish to give up what they referred to as "civilization" in order to go interact or live with them.

An accidental hook up or discovery would be kept close to the vest until the technocracy felt it was appropriate to reveal the data.

UFO: AHAB'S WHITE WHALE

In the original *Watchmen* comic (set in an alternate reality 1985), one of the "heroes" commits what can be considered s a villainous act for the "good of all mankind." He contrives an "alien invasion" so that the United States, the Soviet Union, and the rest of the world will join together in peace and harmony to protect themselves against the outside "alien threat."

If the story rings familiar to some of you, it is because it is based on speeches given by Ronald Reagan in the real world, in which he said an "alien threat" would be the solution to uniting a hostile world.

Numerous "conspiracy theorists", most notably former naval officer William Cooper, the author of the famed underground book *Behold a Pale Horse*, speculated that Reagan's speech was an expositional public "debriefing" to prepare the public to accept a global government as a necessary response to an alien invasion scenario.

Cooper suggested that the US government had been working on a fake alien invasion since the 1930s, and that even Orson Welles' *War of the Worlds* broadcast was an "experiment" to see how the populace would react to such an event.

Cooper hosted a radio talk show, on which he predicted the gradual and pre-planned worldwide economic collapse. Most of his information has proven to be accurate.

William Cooper was eventually gunned down by police officers in front of his Arizona home. What did Cooper know? What were they trying to silence? Even at his most paranoid, he offered what was probably as close to 100% uncompromised, unadulterated human truth as one could possibly find. All of his associates and friends knew that Cooper was legitimate. The Information from his book *Behold a Pale Horse* is, to this day, being revealed as true. However he did say that an alien invasion would happen and that it could be just a psy-op provided by your government.

Well, lately the psy-op — if it is a psy-op — is getting better and better. Skeptics used to always say that with so many cell phones and digital cameras around there would be more UFO "proof" or more documented sightings. Now times have changed and we see more and more so called legitimate sightings recorded on cell phones and digital cameras. There are plenty of people who are now realizing that they can also fake the images with computer software. The unfortunate thing now is that even the skeptics can fake UFO sightings, convince people that they are real and then turn around and reveal how they fooled everyone.

Then they use their fakery as proof that there are no real unidentified flying objects. There are also individuals who are paid to spread disinformation about the subject to cover up secret operations dealing with exotic or secret aircraft. These aircraft are not known to the general public, and they appear to be paranormal.

The UFO is still one big secret and it is being exploited as both real and fake to confuse the public and get them to not be so bold as to reveal what they are seeing or even recording.

Ufology has now become a complicated soap opera of tall tales in short order and short tempers for those who want serious disclosure. There are professional skeptics in bed with the government, some UFO researchers in bed with them as well. The government is also in bed with the Military industrial complex which is allegedly in bed with aliens and it is all there to obfuscate and confuse people into writing it off as some undercover tabloid ruse.

There have been some new cases both in New York and in San Diego where the observer first sees a red orb in the sky. Then there are many red orbs that flash and rotate like a ferris wheel. Then a white strobe appears. It lowers and raises like a probe. Below the red lights there are a string of golden lights.

The UFO is the size of a two story house, or a two story building. The UFO hovers and flashes its lights. It moves slowly and eventually disappears from view.

I have been following reports of his particular UFO since it was reported in Milstadt, Illinois back in the year 2000. A published report of my investigation was found in UFO magazine as a new type of triangular craft was being seen in the Milstadt-Lebanon-St. Louis area and the famous sightings of similar craft in New York, Jerusalem and Utah. These new cases are showing a pattern since the news broke of a UFO over Jerusalem and Utah dropping off a glowing cargo and then flying off into the darkness. After viewing all of the footage from Utah and now from the newest sightings, I am wondering if all of these sightings need to be categorized as a different sighting because of its unconventional size and reports of a strobing probe that is attached to the so called "mothership."

This unique UFO has been my Moby dick of sorts, trying to piece together a phenomenon that is beyond a mere UFO glimpse. These huge ships are rare and are the size of a building.

UFO hunters have pounced on reports of mystery lights in the skies of San Diego and with good reason. A local television news crew snapped the unbelievable UFO above a skyline showing that the object was a huge configuration of red lights a, strobe light and other brilliant lights below.

This strange image of a string of colored flashing lights has been posted an a number of alien and UFO websites after several residents of the city in California, US, reported seeing the same thing.

Local resident Larry Fox sent news channel NBC 7 the picture of an "odd light" he spotted in the night sky.

The channel described the picture as "a string of multi-colored lights." Mr. Fox said he was in his back garden when he saw the strange light to the southwest of the city.

"I ruled out a drone or a plane because the light was stationary. It was a series of flashing lights," he said, adding: "If it was a plane, it would have moved."

Mr. Fox was reported to have described the lights as "red, blue and green" and that they "kept flashing and changing colors."

NBC 7 claimed several other viewers had called in to say they witnessed the same mystery phenomenon, including one of their own photographers, who did not appear to have captured the moment. Days before a similar UFO was seen over Equimalt in British Columbia, however this time the large mothership UFO was releasing smaller probes into the sky that were seen flying around and doing maneuvers. While it was reported that a large UFO had released the objects, authorities all but ruled out a UFO story and decided that what the witnesses saw were drones.

Drones however don't make sonic booms as they travel through the sky and so we see that uncomfortable evidence does not make it into a report that needs to ne revisited to see if there is a pattern.
Any mainstream news expert asked about UFOs should almost certainly be disqualified from having any real opinion on the matter. They only pitch a theory and that is enough to keep things balanced in the view of the news media.

If there is any conspiracy theory or cover-up that can be considered it is that this is a multilevel attempt to construct Intel data about how we react to reports of strange anomalies in the sky. What the public thinks, how disinformation is distributed and how the internet reacts to government agencies and their reports of space threats and then withdrawing their warnings with no accountability.

Allegedly, branches of the military are engaging in psychological warfare involving false flag exercises. These include simulated extraterrestrial attacks. The frightening part is that the military psy-ops groups are conducting these alien-based psychological experiments to test the collective acceptance of a real alien landing. They are allegedly faking occasional UFO reports and YouTube videos to gauge public reaction. They are also allegedly taking real events shown on YouTube and creating a sense of confusion by creating very sophisticated fakes that appear to be eyewitness documentation.

These fakes are used to discredit any and all anomalous events as hoaxes. The mainstream media then takes the story and jokingly ridicules those who believe that the event was out of the ordinary. This has been lost on many armchair skeptics who believe that they know

CGI when they see it. Of course there is CGI; your taxes paid for the intelligence blackouts and disinformation. The psy-op begins and soon everything is a hoax and evidence is overlooked in the race to debunk and not to decipher.

We begin to see a public consensus that has a whiff or a whim claim that any UFO activity is always caused by Project Blue Beam or HAARP. We begin to see every UFO video held to scrutiny because it is assumed by skeptics that people who see lights in the sky are prone to delusions of alien contact. It is also assumed that if the skeptics themselves can fake the evidence, it is almost certainly a hoax created by those who claim to have authentic footage or documentation.

We are now witnessing the hijacking of information by maggot-like thought police.

This type of hijacking of information has created a form of neo-skepticism, in which there is a group of true skeptics who have no knowledge of an external world, or of infinite possibilities. Their whole lives are mired in doubt and contempt for anyone with a belief in something that is beyond the norm. They are adamant in suppressing new ideas and dismissing anything that does not fit into the consensus orthodoxy.

Mankind has been seeded with the idea that his culture and his religious philosophies come from enlightened beings from heaven. The fusing together of science and religion will give mankind a new way to look at the world. Man is set to begin the next step in his evolution and this may be linked to a better understanding of what lies outside the confines of his own planet. There is however a great number of people who will attempt to begin the eschaton or the end times by using whatever means necessary to mold the world to their liking.

I know full well that with new technology leaders, scientists of the world can stage or fake a supernatural, messianic event. They are capable of convincing you of a godlike arrival from heaven.

They can create an extraterrestrial landing, a UFO apocalypse and plant a story, to develop new religious movements. Brainwash scores of individuals in believing in worlds and places where these aliens live. They only need smoke and mirrors to make this happen and an entire world will confess and bow before an image the controllers have created. However there is the other side of the story. Perhaps to our own surprise the faking of such events may just trigger the real thing. That would be an amazing cosmic joke.

THE ALIEN BASE AT POINT DUME

The debate continues over exactly what the truth is behind the sightings of anomalous objects that are above the earth. The U.S. Air Force has explained on many occasions that a lot of what is seen can be explained. However with the obsession of extraterrestrial mythology and reality, every bright light, shooting star, experimental plane, and weather anomaly can end up on the front pages of tabloid newspapers and on special fringe news programs labeled as bonafide extra terrestrial craft with the acronym UFO attached to it.

Special effects wizards can create on a computer grid, creatures that once occupied our darkest nightmares from dinosaurs to slimy tentacled aliens with acidic blood and gnashing teeth.

Ufology lends itself to a variety of theories and that no theory is absolute because it is based primarily on data that is vague. It is vague not because of the evidence in hand but because the casual observer in most cases is not planning on witnessing an event as sporadic as a UFO or supernatural occurrence.

The literature available about UFO's is abundant and the obsession of such topics is evident as we see many people cash in on every new age philosophy and whim. The trouble is that the faith in UFO's and their oogly alien pilots may be premature when you consider that we have thrown all logic off kilter and anthropomorphized many aspects of the possibility of life forms outside of earth.

We are also fixated on the idea that aliens and or UFOs come from outer space when of course there may be a number of these alien craft that may be coming from our oceans and Great lakes.

It is also important to acknowledge the possibility of nature and its ability to continually surprise us with new data and new life that we have overlooked. It is far too tempting to engage in flights of fancy when investigating these miraculous sightings.

Back in 2003 it was reported that scientists probing the Earth's interior found a large reservoir of water equal to the volume of the Arctic Ocean beneath eastern Asia. Just last week Scientists again have reports that they are finding out more about what is under the earth's mantle and what they are finding is more underground ocean located 400 miles beneath Earth's crust

The ocean however is not something that we are familiar with. When we think of ocean water we think of liquid and the typical consistency of ocean water.

This body of water is locked up in a blue mineral called Ringwoodite that lies in the transition zone of hot rock between Earth's surface and core. Interestingly, this water is not in a form familiar to us it's neither liquid, ice nor vapor.

Ringwoodite is the reason this new water us hidden. Its crystal-like structure makes it act like a sponge and draw in hydrogen and trap water.

The new findings may also explain why some earthquakes we experience have a rolling or wavy motion as if water is just below us moving the earth.

This has also sparked even more dialogue about the possibility that the aliens we hear about aren't really extra-terrestrials, but denizens of the deep waters and that they have their bases underwater or on many of the uncharted islands here on earth.

When I was a guest for the television show "Return to the Bermuda Triangle" I had the opportunity to talk with many people that wanted to remind me that much of what is reported about the Bermuda Triangle is natural phenomena, however there also seem to be all sorts of reports of Unidentified Flying objects and Unidentified Submerged Objects. There was also buzz about the naval equivalent of Area 51 known as AUTEC, The Atlantic Undersea Test and Evaluation Center. AUTEC is located at Andros Island right in the middle of the Bermuda triangle. While Naval personnel are open about some things at the facility, the adamantly say that there are no USO's or UFO's there. However sometimes when you bring up AUTEC and USO's and government cover ups some people don't like it.

I took an opportunity to interview Maximillien de Lafayette author UFO-USO and Extraterrestrials of the Sea: Flying Saucers And Aliens Civilizations, Life And Bases Underwater during the time there was speculation of a possible UFO that was underwater in the Baltic. I grilled him on the UFO sightings that were documented during NATO maneuvers in 1952 over the Baltic Sea and their connection to the possible Nazi saucers and the Admiral Byrd reports of underwater bases in the Antarctic from 1947.

On 5 March, 1947 the "El Mercurio" newspaper of Santiago, Chile, had a headline article "On Board the Mount Olympus on the High Seas" which quoted Byrd in an interview with Lee van Atta:

"Adm. Byrd declared today that it was imperative for the United States to initiate immediate defense measures against hostile regions. Furthermore, Byrd stated that he "didn't want to frighten anyone unduly" but that it was "a bitter reality that in case of a new war the continental United

States would be attacked by flying objects which could fly from pole to pole at incredible speeds".

When I brought up these key stories about Operation Mainbrace and Admiral Byrd's operation High Jump, Lafayette abruptly cancelled the interview telling me that I should know why he had to leave and to let my imagination fill in the rest. I was left wondering if he was told by someone or by e-mail that the interview got into territory that he could not touch.

Many stories have been buried regarding UFO's and their relationship to the sea. Their emergence from the liquid medium has gone relatively ignored yet most UFO sightings happen over bodies of water. They descend from the sky and plunge into the sea or the inland lake. This raises the question "Do aliens find refuge in our seas?"

Recently there have been scores of sightings on pacific coast of California. Last January there were so many sightings from Marysville California to Malibu that Peter Davenport from the National UFO reporting center phoned me and told me that they were disrupting power in some areas and cell phone service.

The coast has been experiencing a flap of UFO reports and even the mainstream news has been paying attention to what is happening. On June 20th KABC Channel 7 news in California filed a story about strange lights seen over Malibu and connected it with a story that was actually first reported by Jimmy church of the "Fade to Black" radio show.

The Huffington post reported a few weeks earlier about the possibility of a hidden alien structure below the ocean 6 miles of the coast of Point Dume in Malibu California. It is an unusual looking structure that sits on the seabed floor.

It appears to be an the oval-shaped object that has a huge flat top and what appear to be pillars or columns that seem to reveal the entrance to a darker, inner place.

The anomaly is approximately 2,000 feet below the surface of the water, measuring nearly 3 miles wide.

Jimmy Church the host of Fade To Black on Art Bell's former Dark Matter Radio Network, reported that one of his listeners someone named Maxwell contacted him last month with a Google Earth image showing something odd, underwater off the coast of Malibu. Church then asked graphic designer Dale Romero to capture as many angled images of the anomaly as he could.

The anomaly can be found by using Google earth coordinates 34° 1'23.31"N 118° 59'45.64"W.

Geologists of course are not calling it a UFO base and of course there isn't a sign hanging off of it that declares that it is. Only that in 2009 the anomaly did catch the attention of Geologists and they called it the Sycamore Knoll. Geologists believe that it is a thrust fault and while it is 2000 feet below the surface they aren't about to go down and prove that it is either a natural phenomenon or artificial.

However the pillars and the entrance below is a compelling geological anomaly that can't easily be explained nor can he UFO activity that has been happening near Santa Barbara and strange lights over Venice beach.

The UFO activity may just be a coincidence and there have been many fireballs that are seen that are mistaken for UFO's

However if you do a little research you will find the entire area near Point Dume.

Preston Dennett a MUFON field investigator states that when he began investigating the area in the 1980's he was getting all sorts of information about sightings in the area.

According to Dennett :

Most of these reports came from a certain stretch of California coastline, from about Santa Barbara south to Long Beach. This particular body of

water, I soon learned, had a widespread reputation as a UFO hotspot. After several witnesses told me they believed there was an underwater UFO base there, I decided to conduct a more in-depth investigation to determine the truth. My first step was to survey the research of other prominent investigators. To my surprise, most of the local researchers were already aware of the sightings.

Writes Ann Druffel:

"This body of water lies between the coastlines of Southern California and Santa Catalina Island, 20 miles offshore to the southwest. The area has for at least thirty years been the scene of UFO reports of all kinds: surface sightings of hazy craft which cruise leisurely in full view of military installations, aerial spheres bobbing in oscillating flight, gigantic cloud-cigars, and at least one report of an underwater UFO with uniformed occupants."

Another researcher, Robert Stanley, editor of the now defunct magazine Unicus, writes:

"Even in the sixties, families were going down to the beach and waiting for a UFO to pass by.... By the 1970s, whole families were going down to the beach at Point Dume at night to watch the multi-colored UFOs [that] would sink under the water at times."

MUFON field investigator Bill Hamilton writes:

"For years witnesses have seen many types of UFO cruising off the Palos Verdes Peninsula in Southern California. UFOs have actually been seen to come out of the water in the San Pedro Channel."

I had already uncovered several firsthand cases myself. My next step was to put together a comprehensive list of all the recorded ocean-going encounters in the area.

Dennet came up with more than 50 sighting in the area during his time with MUFON, which begs the question could there be an alien base near Point Dume? Jimmy Church says that investigation will continue.

TRACY CRASH: FALLEN ANGEL

There almost certainly was no Tracy UFO crash ("almost" because it's a little too hot to search the tall grass)- *Taken from the Stockton Record August 7th 1998.*

It was a hot August night in Manteca California and Louis Zamorah was on the Phone with his good Friend Jennifer Lipshin. While he was looking outside he held his breath as he saw something brilliant lighting up the night sky. It was a bluish green fireball. The Fireball creeped across the sky and then sped up. It made no sound that he could hear. At first he thought he was seeing a firework darting across the sky until he noticed another fireball separating from the first looking as if it were playing tag with it. He thought he saw something come up from the ground like a bolt of lightning and the ball disappeared near the area of a school. He braced himself for the sound of an explosion or a crash, but he heard nothing. Only the deafening silence of the night. He told his friend Jennifer that he saw something strange. He told her of its odd movement. Jennifer wondered if maybe Louis was witness to a UFO.

I was working late on my computer and saw that I had received and e-mail. The e-mail was from some broadcast buddies who worked at another Citadel communications radio station in Reno. Since Ground Zero is broadcast on KBER another Citadel station they thought that maybe I would be interested in a UFO story. I thought they were kidding me, and usually I don't jump on UFO stories unless other people more qualified like Peter Davenport investigate them or if I receive more than one report.

Well this was one of the exceptions to the rule. I received 3 reports. I had said to the guys at Earthbroadcasting that we might have a UFO down near San Francisco and this time it is a clear case. It has made the mainstream press. I took for granted that the press could give us the real story. I was wrong. After reporting the possible downing of a UFO on EarthMail.

I contacted Olav Phillips from the S4 Database at 2A.M. This was the first time I actually had called him. We had been in contact over the net, but this time I felt it was my duty to personally inform him of the situation.

He told me that he had searched the News organizations for the story and couldn't find a thing. I told him that there must be something because people are calling KCBS asking about UFO's over San Francisco. He told me that there was nothing on the wire.

I clicked to the Art Bell web site and looked to see if Art had been notified. Art was having one of his "Call me if you are an alien" shows and so he didn't mention anything. I was stumped. If 3 reports came to me, and KCBS reported it, and if KOH in Reno saw the UFO, then why is there no more news?

I called Olav and told him to call Peter Davenport of the National UFO reporting Center in Washington State. Peter said that there was no report of any UFO activity over San Francisco.

I felt like I had been hoaxed. I was ready to recant the report and say that I had egg on my face. It had to have been a huge meteor. I then received a report from Claude DiDomenica from the UFO Network that a UFO had been shot down over Tracy California. The UFO was brought down by some sort of Laser Technology near Lawrence Livermore Labs. I then was thinking that maybe a foreign plane tried to fly over or attack San Francisco and ended up 300 miles away from its destination and was shot down by a tracer bullet. There were so many possibilities that I thought of every single one. Each idea I posted on my website including the chance that an SR-71 was testing a LASRE cone engine. Another e-mail came from Claude. Some one had suggested that we pray for the entities that may have died in the Crash over Tracy and I then realized that the story had been tainted. The word UFO has been prematurely characterized as a flying saucer with little green men inside. The minute you talk of Alien grays dying, the media will want to focus on the weirdness of the event. They will discredit it and become cynical. This wasn't going to be easy to report , and the investigation will stop with the paper boy throwing the morning paper in the bushes. But if there were "close encounters" to report, it should be handled with the same respect as "sexual encounters" in the Whitehouse which can equally be described as "tabloid."

The Next day Olav sent me a report that he got out of a San Francisco paper that talks about the strange lights seen over the bay. It was probably the only printed piece that actually addressed the lights in the sky. The paper reported a meteor, however the words "most likely" were used. Meaning in my opinion that they did not even attempt to check. It felt as though that there was an inconsistency in reports from eyewitnesses and the press. The hysteria in some areas did not match the press reports. It was also inconsistent that most UFO oriented shows knew nothing about the case. This is how I think. When something reeks of inconsistency I jump on it to learn more. Even if the press says "case closed." My hunches have been right in the past, but this was a huge gamble. It just seemed strange. Why was there a news blackout? I just didn't buy the "Everyone wants to see a UFO argument." None of the reports I received at first said anything about a flying saucer. We even posted a logical explanation of what might have happened and yet it was still concluded that what people saw was a meteor. Then the alien reports came in and then I realized we didn't have a prayer. But I did not give up.

On August 7th a report was filed in the Stockton Record reporting the Internet interest in the possible UFO crash over Tracy California. I was even quoted, because I had commented on the possibility of an experimental aircraft being tested near Lawrence Livermore labs. I also was not discounting the possibility of something extra-terrestrial but the reality is that it is highly improbable in most cases. The report in the Stockton Record made light of any possibility other than a meteor. This angered me because there was no objectivity. I knew then that no one bothered to do any listening or any homework.

I received E-mail from a Tracy resident. He told me that he was very curious at the fact that security had been beefed up near Lawrence

Livermore labs and that some black vehicles were seen in the area with a Flat bed Truck. This reminded me of another case that happened in Kecksburg , Pennsylvania in December of 1965. A fireball streaked across Lake Erie and crash-landed in Kecksburg. The fireball was first reported as a meteor. But the real story went virtually unreported. What wasn't reported was the thousands of UFO reports that clearly stated that what streaked across the sky left a smoke trail that was visible for 20 minutes, yet the press still reported it as a meteor. Townspeople however were terrified about the incident. Many claimed that an acorn shaped object with strange writing on it was in a small crater. The military took over the town and put the object on a flatbed truck and covered it. The Truck was escorted through town and many believe it was some sort of extra-terrestrial craft.

I decided to contact Jennifer Lipshin. Her Friend Louis Zamorah was a witness to the lights. I wanted to see what exactly happened. Jennifer was surprised that I still was interested in the case because of the news reports. I told her that there were some inconsistencies that needed to be investigated. I asked about all that was reported and she said that she wasn't sure because Louis was very excited. He was spooked about what he saw and kept quiet about the incident. She gave me his number and I called him. Louis told me that it was the strangest thing he ever saw. That he didn't believe the papers. The Manteca resident believes that he saw something that was being intelligently flown. He estimated that whatever it was it was about 2000 feet in the air and about the size of two Volkswagen automobiles. He claims that it zoomed and then slowed down and then something shot at it. The bluish green ball turned and then separated. One other light moved to the side of it. Fell behind and followed it behind a school. He said that the strange thing was that there wasn't an explosion. He did comment that after all of the commotion that there were a few Jets flying over that ripped a hole in the silence. He then commented that there was a helicopter that flew overhead.

After the witnesses gave me their stories, I started believing the conclusion that perhaps there may have been a meteor over the skies in Tracy. The whole story seemed so perfect so classic that I was sensing a too good to be true attitude. I estimated something that big would have put a crater in the ground. Something that bright had to have caused a fire. I also concluded that if there was a crash of anything, there had to be some kind of crew trying to recover the plane or the saucer if there was one. We had reports of a recovery crew, but it was your classic X-files type of scenario. I thought that is story is so good , why am I the only one reporting it? I received a newspaper report that said that a tire fire had broken out in Tracy. 7 million tires were ablaze . Tire fires are the worst fires of all. They cause black smoke and they are seldom put out. Some burn for months. That is when I decided that this smoke screen was a convenient smoke screen. Whenever there is something out of the ordinary there is always something to screw up the investigation. This Tire fire was it. No one could see the ground from the air. No one could get near the area, and people were warned to stay indoors. If hazardous material personelle were on the scene to take soil samples of an ET crash site so one know. If they pulled bodies out of an alien spacecraft no one would see. If they recovered an exotic craft who would want to get near a tire fire?

The circumstantial evidence was so overwhelming that I changed my mind about the Tracy "meteor". Something crashed there. Something was retrieved, and it had something to do with Lawrence Livermore Labs.

A fax was sent to me from someone who claimed to have some information about the Tracy crash. The fax claimed that it was derived from naval information. It said there was no crash. There was however a TAV. I did not know what a TAV was, so I poked around and asked my military consultants. They told me that TAV stood for Trans Atmospheric vehicle. The Vehicle was heading for Los Angeles. According to the Fax it moved Mach 60. It was at 160,000 feet and descended. It was engaged by F-18's over the Bay area. They allegedly fired KKV's (Kinetic Kill Vehicles) at the "unknown" The craft then headed towards Lawrence Livermore Labs and was engaged again. It was hit and a piece of it had blown off. This would be congruent with the eyewitness testimony. I later learned the KKV's were laser weapons which would explain Lawrence Livermore, a facility that specializes in Laser and Super collider technology. However there was no proof that this had a connection. It was just a coincidence.

So there it was, a classic UFO story, with strange lights, eyewitness testimony, secret reports, and something to cover the tracks of covert activities.

After we reported the information on The Ground Zero show, people all over the world heard the story about the Tracy crash. I received letters from so many people saying that I was chasing a falsehood. That the media said it was meteor. Well I guess they have the final word on everything. They have more money than I do and they have a newspaper. That makes them right. But would a reporter go all the way out to Tracy in 112-degree heat to chase after alien grays? If they were believers, yes but most reporters don't believe in alien mythology. Some won't even bother to file a report. I was lucky I knew people from Modesto. I knew someone, who was heading out there for the weekend, I told him to snoop around for me. He did. He brought back another strange coincidence.

Silas Royster the owner of the Tire Dump in Tracy died of cancer. After I had heard the news, I felt that this story was getting weirder by the day. I felt that the Ground Zero show would be the last word on the subject. We had all the information on the table. I was wrong.

I received a letter from someone who told me that there would be more information coming out of Tracy regarding the UFO crash and that my investigation did not include the possibility of reverse engineering of Extra terrestrial craft. I guess because there was no proof of an Alien space craft only circumstantial evidence. Now the evidence suggests that yes there was something that was seen over Tracy. It may have been extra-terrestrial. It's an outrageous leap of faith but there is a pattern. A classic pattern that has been spoken of before. This story sounds so familiar. After a month passed the classic ending was announced to the press.

Lawrence Livermore National Laboratory recently announced that they had the plans for a new aircraft design, dubbed ``Hyper Soar'', that could fly at about 6,700 mph, or Mach 10,and would experience far less heat build-up on its airframe than previous aircraft designs of it's type. Preston Carter, the Livermore aerospace engineer who developed the Hyper Soar concept says that the craft will be able to travel at 130, 000 feet at Mach 10.

Carter said to the press that the key to Hyper Soar would be its ``skipping'' motion along the edge of Earth's atmosphere, much as a rock is skipped across water. It would make it possible to travel to Japan from the Midwest in about an hour and a half.

This new information is explained it all. While most of the area news ignored witnesses and developed a story of their own, Ground Zero stuck by its story. This does not rule out the Alien spacecraft theory. Not by a long shot.

Did Lawrence Livermore recover pieces from an exotic Craft near Tracy California, and did they reverse engineer this craft in order to come up with the new plans for Hyper Soar?

This fits all of the classic stories. Kenneth Arnold who saw a strange formation of craft "skipping" across the skies in 1947. A little over a week later the Roswell incident took place.

It was reported that the Army-airforce had a flying saucer. There were also reports that crews were sent in to retrieve alien bodies, and that the wreckage of the saucer was sent to Dayton Ohio to be analyzed. The story was then removed and it was reported that a Weather Balloon had crashed. Totally discrediting eyewitnesses. It was soon after that, the Army and the airforce separated. Supersonic jets came on the scene and man was finding himself moving faster through the skies.

The Late Lieutenant Phillip Corso claims that the Roswell crash yielded remarkable technology from alien sources, that it was reverse engineered and we see the results of the reverse technology today.

Another man who made claims of reverse Alien technology is Physicist Bob Lazar, who you may remember claims he was called in to reverse engineer exotic craft at the S4 base near Area 51.

He Claimed that the craft he saw would rise up and then the craft would go into a roll. Then the engines were focused on a small area. They were fired and the ship would move in a skipping motion through space. Hyper soar is said to be able to soar 130,000 feet just outside the atmosphere, then it would turn off its air breathing engine and coast back to the edge of the atmosphere and then skip back into space.

Once again another coincidence. Too many coincidences in this story. I cannot go completely on the record and state a perfect knowledge of what happened over Tracy. Only you can make up your own mind.

Here is what it looks like. An Alien or foreign spacecraft was near Tracy. It was shot at. Pieces of it fell off. A government Lab recovered them. A fire may have been set to keep people from the area. A man who owned the property that was burning died. The fire was not put out for a month. Enough time to clear the area and analyze what may have fallen out of the sky. Technicians may or may not have reverse engineered the pieces. They now have the plans for a new plane. Lawrence Livermore is now in the Trans Atmospheric Vehicle business.

The authorities say it was a meteor. Therefore the consensus reality has concluded it was a meteor. Officially. We stuck with the possibility of an experimental craft. Something tells me it was more than that.

Was it? You have the evidence. Keep your mind at GROUND ZERO and then you decide.

About Clyde Lewis

Clyde is a powerful voice in parapolitical and paranormal news and commentary. With a diverse background in news, acting, writing and radio, he entertains and captivates audiences across multiple platforms. Lewis' career in radio began in Utah in 1982 and he created Ground Zero in 1995 in Salt Lake City. Lewis has produced Ground Zero programs online, on radio and on television. The program (which takes its name from the scientific definition of the term) joined FM News 101 KXL in 2011 and consistently ranks #1 in the market.

Lewis has appeared in a SHOWTIME special with magicians Penn & Teller, as well as the television programs Sightings, Strange Universe and the Discovery Channel special Return to the Bermuda Triangle. He has been published in both UFO Magazine and Unknown Magazine, and has been featured in Rolling Stone. Lewis is the model for characters in such books as Safe House by Andrew Vachss, Supernatural Law by Batton Lash, and Alien Invasion by Michael Tresca.

A fan of B-horror and science-fiction movies, comic books and mythology, Lewis has also published his own fanzines and co-written scripts for television and radio. He appeared in the movies Nightfall, which he co-wrote with director Kevin Delullo; Cage in Box Elder; and Citizen Toxie: The Toxic Avenger Part IV, in which he provided the voice of the title character.

Currently, Lewis is working with lawyer and P.I. Galen Cook on the investigation of the latest suspect in the D.B. Cooper case, Wolfgang Gossett, a one-time associate of Lewis' and a new suspect in the mysterious case.

Clyde currently lives in Portland, Oregon.

Made in the USA
San Bernardino, CA
19 May 2018